T0319097

Elements in the Economics of Emerging Markets
edited by
Bruno S. Sergi
Harvard University

DIAGNOSING HUMAN CAPITAL AS A BINDING CONSTRAINT TO GROWTH

Tests, Symptoms, and Prescriptions

Miguel Angel Santos
Center for International Development at Harvard University
School of Public Policy, London School of Economics

Farah Hani
Center for International Development at Harvard University

CAMBRIDGE
UNIVERSITY PRESS

University Printing House, Cambridge CB2 8BS, United Kingdom

One Liberty Plaza, 20th Floor, New York, NY 10006, USA

477 Williamstown Road, Port Melbourne, VIC 3207, Australia

314–321, 3rd Floor, Plot 3, Splendor Forum, Jasola District Centre, New Delhi – 110025, India

103 Penang Road, #05–06/07, Visioncrest Commercial, Singapore 238467

Cambridge University Press is part of the University of Cambridge.

It furthers the University's mission by disseminating knowledge in the pursuit of education, learning, and research at the highest international levels of excellence.

www.cambridge.org
Information on this title: www.cambridge.org/9781108971591
DOI: 10.1017/9781108975223

© Miguel Angel Santos and Farah Hani 2021

First published 2021

A catalogue record for this publication is available from the British Library.

ISBN 978-1-108-97159-1 Paperback
ISSN 2631-8598 (online)
ISSN 2631-858X (print)

Diagnosing Human Capital as a Binding Constraint to Growth

Tests, Symptoms, and Prescriptions

Elements in the Economics of Emerging Markets

DOI: 10.1017/9781108975223
First published online: November 2021

Miguel Angel Santos
Center for International Development at Harvard University
School of Public Policy, London School of Economics

Farah Hani
Center for International Development at Harvard University

Author for correspondence: Miguel Angel Santos,
miguel_santos@hks.harvard.edu

Abstract: The empirical literature on the contributions of human capital investments to economic growth shows mixed results. While evidence from Organization for Economic Co-operation and Development (OECD) countries demonstrates that human capital accumulation is associated with growth accelerations, the substantial efforts of developing countries to improve access to and quality of education, as a means for skill accumulation, did not translate into higher income per capita. In this Element, we propose a framework, building on the principles of Growth Diagnostics, to enable practitioners to determine whether human capital investments are a priority for a country's growth strategy. We then discuss and exemplify different tests to diagnose human capital in a place, drawing on the Harvard Growth Lab's experience in different development contexts, and discuss various policy options to address skill shortages.

Keywords: human capital, skills, economic growth, Growth Diagnostics, developing countries

ISBNs: 9781108971591 (PB), 9781108975223 (OC)
ISSNs: 2631-8598 (online), 2631-858X (print)

Contents

Introduction

Common wisdom along the hallways of development agencies preaches the importance of human capital for development, whereas one of the most important issues policy-makers in developing countries often face is unemployment among educated youth. While evidence from Organization for Economic Co-operation and Development (OECD) countries shows that human capital accumulation is associated with growth accelerations, the massive efforts to improve access to and quality of schooling in developing countries have not translated, on average, into higher income per capita. Moreover, cross-country differences in schooling per worker and output per capita have moved in opposite directions, with the near-universal expansion in schooling reducing the former while per capita income gaps widened.[1] How do we reconcile these seemingly contradictory positions? Is the problem that some developing countries have a relative abundance of skills, but other constraints are preventing these from being demanded and utilized? Is it that schooling is not producing skills so that there is demand for human capital that existing schooling and training programs do not meet? Or is it instead that there is demand for human capital and relative abundance skills, but labor market failures are preventing skilled people from being hired? In this Element, we argue that the answer to this puzzle depends on country-specific factors and propose a framework to assess whether improvements in a country's human capital can reasonably be expected to have an impact on economic growth.

When can we expect improvements in the provision of a factor – human capital – to be good for growth? Solow (1956) proposed modeling and studying economic output as a production function with complementary inputs: physical capital and labor, and a productivity factor that depends on the level of technological progress. Mankiw, Romer, and Weil (1992) introduced an augmented model by incorporating the notion of human capital. The model assumes diminishing returns to capital – as capital accumulation increases, the incentive to save and invest in capital decreases – leading to a level of income per capita that is determined by savings rates, population growth, and technological progress, all exogenous variables. Under these assumptions, growth in output per capita is exogenous: any permanent increases in the provision of a production factor will lead to temporary positive growth rates that allow the income level to shift permanently. The economic growth delivered thereby can only be transitional in nature. Within this context, investments in the stock of human capital yield a shift in income level but do not boost growth.

---

[1] See Pritchett (2006).

Escaping Solow invariance and the exogeneity of growth requires an endogenous growth engine and relaxing the assumption of diminishing returns. Romer (1986) proposed a growth model of endogenous technological change, expanding the concept of factor accumulation as a determinant of growth from physical and human capital to include knowledge. The accumulation of knowledge leads to externalities – as knowledge is non-rivalrous in nature – and thereby exhibits increasing returns to scale. Hence, growth in output per capita is no longer a temporary and exogenous phenomenon but rather the product of knowledge accumulation by profit-maximizing agents and as such can increase over time. Within this context, investments in human capital may have a significant impact on long-run growth if they are related to the production, adoption, and diffusion of knowledge.

A policy implication of Romer's model is that knowledge can be transferred to developing countries as blueprints, and the only constraint to economic growth is the speed of physical and human capital accumulation. Yet, by the early 2000s, economic growth outcomes of developing countries showed income divergence in most regions except for East Asia and South Asia, mostly due to the slow or lack of convergence of total factor productivity (Bosworth and Collins, 2003). Decades of standard growth accounting exercises between 1960 and 2000 show that capital accumulation – physical or human – only partially explains the cross-country output gap (Hall and Jones, 1999; Bils and Klenow, 2000; Caselli, 2005).

The Growth Diagnostics framework introduced by Hausmann, Rodrik, and Velasco (2008) argues for the prioritization of growth reforms contingent on a country's economic environment. They propose a simple model in which economic growth is determined by the returns on factor accumulation, the appropriability of these returns and the costs of financing factor accumulation. Within this context, distortions on the provision of the underlying production factors constrain investment and growth. The distortion with the highest estimated growth yield is called the most binding constraint and shall be prioritized within the allocation of policy attention and government resources. The range of factors that underlie the economic growth process is broad, including finance, infrastructure, human capital, macroeconomic and microeconomic risks, and market failures.

We build on the principles of Growth Diagnostics proposed by Hausmann, Rodrik, and Velasco (2008) and propose a framework to investigate and assess *whether improvements in the accumulation of human capital shall be prioritized to accelerate economic growth in a specific country.* We illustrate the application of the framework by drawing on Harvard University's Growth Lab's fifteen years of experience in applying Growth Diagnostics at the national and sub-national levels worldwide. We demonstrate the deployment of four principles of differential diagnosis to test whether human capital is the most binding constraint. Practitioners will find in this Element a combination of econometric tests, characteristics of the data required and proposed visualizations for their results, as well as more descriptive calculations derived from data available through various enterprise surveys, international financial institutions, or other publicly available sources. Additionally, we take stock of common policy interventions aimed at alleviating or overcoming distortions in cases where human capital is diagnosed as the most binding constraint.

The Element is organized as follows. Section 1 reviews the evolution of the concept of human capital in the economic literature, contrasts definitions against recent research outputs on schooling – an avenue to acquire human capital – in developing countries, and proposes a framework to assess the adequacy of human capital to support the process of economic growth in a specific country. Section 2 describes the four diagnostic principles to assess the adequacy of the human capital supply and access to it, as well as illustrates their use through examples from national and sub-national contexts. In doing so, we consider means to acquire human capital that are different from schooling: On-the-job training and experience can account for skill accumulation in ways that are not captured by schooling alone. Section 3 provides guidance on distilling the analysis results to judge whether human capital is indeed a binding constraint to growth and formulate policies that governments may adopt to overcome shortages in the supply of human capital. Conclusions, limitations, and potential avenues for further applied research work are presented in Section 4.

1 What Is Human Capital?

The term *capital* has traditionally referred to assets generated through a deliberate investment and whose operation is associated with a return. The most obvious forms of capital are physical and financial assets. The notion of human skills and knowledge as a form of capital, while alluded to by Adam Smith as early as 1776 (Smith, 1776), was formalized by pivotal contributions from Schultz, Becker, and Mincer in the late 1950s and early 1960s, which gave rise to a literature that sought to define the concept and study the return on investments in human capital.

Schultz (1960) defined human capital as the skills and knowledge that constitute an individual's productive capacity and ought to be treated as capital, since individuals in jobs apply their abilities and "provide a productive service of value to the economy (p. 571)." As such, human capital formation, through schooling and training, promised positive growth-promoting externalities making human capital essential for economic development (Myrdal, 1957; Schultz, 1960). Schultz also emphasized the need to understand the return on investment in human capital and, ultimately, how it contributes to national income. Building on this literature, Schultz (1960, 1961, 1963) and Lucas (1988) extended the neoclassical economic growth model to incorporate human capital as a cumulative factor contributing to economic productivity and growth, beyond manual labor and similar to physical capital. In these models, individuals' human capital affects not only their own productivity but also that of other factors.

In parallel, the contributions of Becker and Mincer provided the foundational frameworks and methods to measure the return on schooling and other human capital investments. Becker (1962) argued that some activities affect future individual well-being rather than the present, by "embedding" individuals with resources that impact their future real earnings. He proposed a theory connecting "investments in human capital" to worker earnings, which would increase with the value of investments in skill accumulation, on or out of the job. Becker and Chiswick (1966) provided empirical estimates of the return to different levels of schooling on earnings. Mincer (1958, 1974, 1984) contributed empirical models to measure the effects of skills accumulation – with schooling and work experience as proxies – on income distributions.

Schooling and on-the-job training are the most common forms of human capital investment. Other investments that contribute to productivity include physical and mental healthcare, nutrition, other means of acquiring knowledge or information, or noncognitive skills (Becker, 1962). Healthcare and nutrition are critical to build cognitive abilities and keep individuals engaged in economic activities beneficial for them and their societies. The impact of deteriorating health on human well-being and the economy has been studied (Rosen, 1988; Becker, 2007) and echoed stronger than ever in the wake of the COVID-19 pandemic. Interestingly, Schultz (1961) also discusses migration, particularly internal relocations where individuals migrate from rural to urban areas to benefit from job opportunities, as a form of investment in human capital. Under this view, individuals incur a "cost of migration" to be able to employ their human capital in opportunities in the destination. These opportunities, over their lifetime, will generate a larger return than in the location of origin and compensate for the costs associating to migration.

Before we proceed to discuss a framework to determine whether policy interventions aimed at augmenting human capital shall be the priority to accelerate growth in a specific country, we note three points regarding human capital accumulation and economic growth.

First, despite near-universal school enrollment achieved as part of the international drive to promote schooling under the second Millennium Development Goal, evidence suggests that little human capital was created to generate literacy, let alone provide children with skills and knowledge. Pritchett (2013) documents extensively the paradox that while the average years of schooling in the developing world went from two years in 1950 to seven years in 2010, the poor quality of schooling worldwide had not led to *education* or learning. Assessments from several developing countries, such as India, Indonesia, Pakistan, Nigeria, and Peru, show that students' learning outcomes in these countries lag those of students in OECD countries. Kaffenberger and Pritchett (2017) study the learning profiles of young adults between eighteen and thirty-seven years of age in ten developing countries to examine the association between schooling completion and learning outcomes. They find that in six out of the ten countries, half or more than half of young adults who completed primary schooling cannot read a few sentences without assistance. Moreover, according to a 2017 survey of learning outcomes of youth between fourteen and eighteen years old in rural communities in India carried by ASER Centre,[2] 45 percent of those enrolled in tertiary education were not able to tell the time (Look Beyond Basics: Annual Status Education Report, 2017). In short, there has been a lot of schooling in the developing world but no accumulation of human capital, in any of the senses implied by the set of definitions previously reviewed.

Second, it goes without saying that investing in human capital may carry numerous noneconomic or nonmonetary benefits. Increasingly, the international development agenda has emphasized and sought to study the impact of investments in human capital on a broad range of life outcomes (United Nations Economic Commission for Europe, 2016). For example, investing in women's schooling is expected to positively influence their own well-being and that of their families. Kaffenberger and Pritchett (2020) leverage cross-national data on schooling and assess literacy to compare the association of child mortality, fertility, women's empowerment with women's literacy (i.e., learning resulting from schooling) versus schooling (assuming schooling often does not translate into literacy). Not surprisingly, they find the associations to be larger than initially estimated when using schooling levels only – not adjusted for learning. An important implication of this study is that the life or nonmonetary

---

[2] ASER Centre is an autonomous assessment, survey, evaluation, and research unit within the Pratham network.

impact to schooling as an investment in human capital depends on the transmission mechanism through which it generates the benefit. The study points toward learning – that is, the effectiveness of the investment at generating human capital.

Third, in line with the previous two points and also with the Growth Diagnostics framework, empirical evidence from developing countries demonstrates that the marginal return to schooling was lower than expected in many countries (Temple, 1999; Pritchett, 2006). Higher levels of schooling did not translate into higher levels of national development or human well-being. Figure 1 compares cross-country schooling levels and income per capita across four different countries. The data show convergence in schooling with a divergence in income. While schooling levels in Ghana, Thailand, and Mexico were much lower than in a more developed country like France before 1970, these countries (and many other developing countries) witnessed an expansion in schooling after 1970. By 2005, Mexico's level of schooling was similar to that of France in 1995. Ghana was not much further behind. Thailand showed the least progress among this group of countries – by 2005, it achieved the 1985 and 2000 level of schooling of France and Ghana, respectively. Yet comparing the countries' per capita income levels shows a massive boom in income per capita in Thailand, which comes with an improvement in the country's socioeconomic indicators. Yet Ghana's income per capita stagnated.

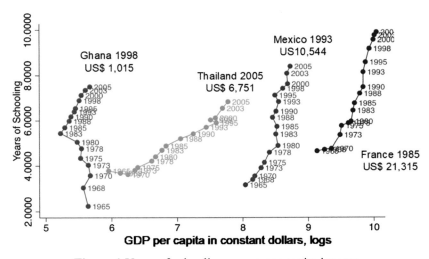

Figure 1 Years of schooling versus per capita income
Source: World Development Indicators

Human Capital as a Binding Constraint to Growth: A Framework

For the purposes of this Element, we will adopt different definitions of human capital at the individual and the country levels. *The human capital of an individual refers to the physical and cognitive capabilities, acquired through schooling and training, that allow individuals to increase the productivity of their efforts. Consequently, a country's human capital is the spectrum of skills available through its working-age population.* The skill spectrum enables economic activities, the adoption of new technologies, and the development of new products and services, which are all tightly linked to the process of economic growth.

The starting point of a Growth Diagnostic exercise is a growth model with different distortions leading to two potential problems constraining investments: (1) low expected private returns to asset accumulation and (2) high cost of finance (Hausmann, Klinger, and Wagner, 2008). Potential constraints to growth coming from human capital fall under the former: firms might be hesitant to carry out investment as the expected returns are low due to low levels of human capital. As such, the question of whether human capital is a binding constraint to growth refers to whether the skill spectrum *in the country* is adequate and accessible to firms looking to make a return on their investment.

Figure 2 lays out the framework to study the motivating question: Do firms have access to adequate skills to invest and generate competitive returns? Firms might not be investing because (1) the stock of skills in the country is inadequate, (2) they are unable to access available skills due to misallocations, or (3) the cost or risk associated with hiring needed skills is high. Constraints (1) and (2) can be characterized as problems of low social returns on investments because the needed skills are not available in the economy or are not accessible to high-growth potential sectors and firms. That is, firms expect a low return on their investment due to a shortage of needed skills. Low levels of human capital or inadequate spectrum of skills might hinder returns because either they prevent firms from operating at the frontier of their production possibilities (forcing them to be less efficient) or firms have to bid up for scarce skills, and this renders their returns less competitive when compared to other potential locations.

Constraint (3) is a problem of appropriability, where firms' ability to privately appropriate the returns to their investment is low due to microeconomic risks, such as, labor market rigidities like binding minimum wage or employment regulations that reduce firms' ability to generate an acceptable return on their investment.

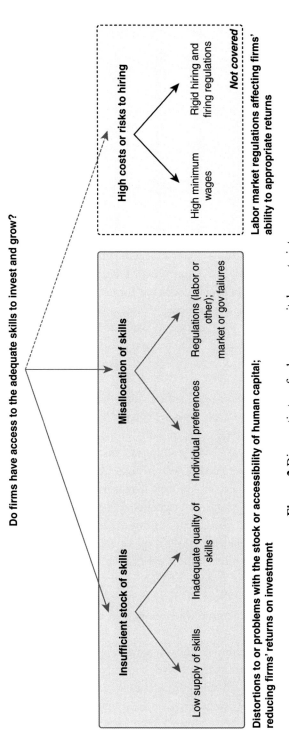

Figure 2 Diagnostic tree for human capital constraints

In this Element, we focus on the problem of low social return (constraints [1] and [2]) and leave out appropriability problems (constraint [3]), as the latter requires a different set of diagnostic tools and policy strategies.

We define constraint (1) – insufficient stock of skills – to be a shortage in the quantity or poor quality of skills supplied to meet existing demand. We define constraint (2) – misallocation of skills – as a mismatch or limited firm access to available skills. Several country-specific institutions, rules, regulations, or norms can lead to the misallocation of skills. For example, cultural norms leading women to work in traditional and culturally "acceptable" occupations or young talent queueing for public sector employment might deprive economic activities of needed skills and possibly hinder human capital accumulation in the country. Other sources of misallocation include labor regulations such as professional licensing rules creating barriers to entry to certain occupations or outright exclusion of foreign labor from certain occupations that are reserved for nationals. Market failures can also lead to the misallocation of skills across sectors or geographies: here, the extensive margin of labor supply constrains investments in potential sectors and poses as fixed cost preventing the emergence of potential sectors (Blundell, Bozio, and Laroque, 2011; Michau, 2011).

Finally, it is necessary to reiterate that under the Growth Giagnostics framework, the question of whether human capital is the most binding constraint to growth cannot be answered in isolation. A country's skill spectrum exists along with other complementary factors that enable its deployment in economic activities. As such, the conclusion on the binding constraint must be made in relative terms, after diagnosing other complementary factors. Human capital only becomes a binding constraint to growth when it is relatively scarcer than the supply of other complementary factors and capabilities.

2 Testing for Human Capital as a Binding Constraint to Growth

Hausmann, Klinger, and Wagner (2008) propose four principles of differential diagnosis to establish whether a factor is a binding constraint to private investment and economic growth. Is the factor's price high, signaling higher relative scarcity? Would a relaxation in the constraint be associated with an increase in private investment and growth? Are firms that rely on the factor more intensively less prevalent than those that do not? Are there firms attempting to bypass the potential constraint? (Table 1). These four signals aim to reveal whether private firms are incurring high costs or facing distortions in securing the supply of certain production inputs. This section is devoted to illustrating how to deploy these diagnostic signals to test whether human capital is the binding constraint.

Table 1 The four diagnostic signals

Diagnostic signal: if human capital is a binding constraint to growth	Description
The shadow price of human capital should be high; there should be high-wage premiums for skilled workers.	• High Actual or implied market prices (wages) • A high shadow price implies that relieving the constraint would have a large impact on private investment.
Changes in the stock of human capital should be associated to changes in private investment and growth.	• If a human capital is a binding constraint to investment or growth, relaxing the constraint should be associated with incremental private investments or growth.
Agents attempting to overcome or bypass skill shortages.	• Agents in the economy are likely responding to the constraint through various interventions or investments to circumvent human capital shortages.
Camels and Hippos: Agents less intensive in human capital are more likely to thrive (and vice versa).	• Sectors that rely more intensely on human capital should be less prevalent or have a relatively lower contribution to exports, value added, or employment than sectors that those that do not.

Note: Authors' adaptation is based on the principles of Hausmann, Klinger, and Wagner (2008).

Before we jump into testing the four diagnostic signals, a natural starting point in our quest would be to examine the characteristics of the labor market against comparable countries. A thorough understanding of the demographics, employment trends, schooling, and quality of education would help frame the results of our empirical tests within the specifics of the country's labor market.

Demographics

It is important to start the Growth Diagnostic exercise by framing the question of growth and human capital in the larger context of the country under study.

A great point to start is portraying the trajectories of growth and human capital: evolution of birth rates, fertility rates, mortality, dependency ratios, and literacy rates. Observing the evolution of these indicators with respect to the income level, and comparing the country's position vis-à-vis its peers, can be informative regarding the relative evolution of the socioeconomic dynamics within the place of interest.

The World Bank's Human Capital Index (World Bank, 2020) measures the amount of human capital an individual in a given country can achieve. The index allows a benchmarking comparison of relevant health and education indicators across countries and can be a useful starting point to contextualize the human capital profile of the country of interest.

Employment

Labor market outcomes can help paint an initial picture of the relative supply and demand of skills in the economy. What are the characteristics of those who are employed versus those who are unemployed? How is the labor force distributed across sectors and occupations? These questions help to characterize the supply of skills and are ideally answered differentiating by education level and considering specific dimensions that are relevant for the particular country (gender, age, citizenship, and indigenous origins).

If human capital were a binding constraint due to the limited availability of specific skills, one would expect to see the employment levels in that category of skills to be exceptionally high. On the contrary, high unemployment may suggest low demand for those skills. Yet low demand may be due to the low quality of graduates in domestic colleges; hence, this signal by itself is not sufficient to dismiss the constraint. Analyzing patterns of employment among immigrant workers might be a fertile source of additional evidence. For example, a large concentration of foreigners across high-skill jobs, coupled with low employment rates or low wages for skilled domestic workers, is a stronger indicator of the inadequacy of the local supply of skills.

If human capital were a binding constraint due to misallocation of skills across sectors, one would expect to see a sharp segmentation of the labor force, with one or more groups concentrated in few sectors, staying out of the labor force or out of specific sectors. For example, it is a common feature in some developing countries that citizens prefer public employment to private employment because of job security, social protection, or higher relative wages. Additionally, social norms might restrict women's participation in the labor force to a few sectors seen as "acceptable for women" (Kasoolu et al., 2019).

Labor market segmentation may indicate obstacles to employment and further accumulation of human capital as firms struggle to recruit needed skills.

Schooling Quantity and Quality

In terms of schooling, one condition for human capital to be a constraint is the low supply of skills – relative to demand. The availability of skills can be proxied by a population's years of schooling and the quality of education. Increasingly, skill measurement surveys are becoming available to assess particular skills, such as numerical, of working populations (*Comisión Nacional de Productividad*, 2016).

We look at the example of Mexico's poorest state: Chiapas. It is located at the southernmost of Mexico and is most known for the Zapatista rebellion, an uprising carried by more than 3,000 indigenous people in the early morning of January 1, 1994 – on the very same day, the North American Free Trade Agreement became effective. Chiapas has the third-largest share (27 percent) of individuals speaking an indigenous language among all Mexican federal entities, after neighboring states Oaxaca (34 percent) and Yucatan (30 percent).[3]

If we were to understand whether human capital is the binding constraint to growth in Chiapas, we could start off by displaying the schooling distribution of the labor force in the state vis-à-vis the rest of Mexico. According to the panels shown in Figure 3, the labor force in Chiapas is less educated than in the rest of the country by a significant margin. By 2010, the average Mexican worker had 2.2 more years of schooling than a worker in Chiapas. The breach shows up at different levels of schooling. According to the 2010 Population Census, the share of illiterate people in Chiapas that year was more than twice that in the rest of Mexico (16% vs. 6%); the share of individuals with zero schooling was also more than twice as large (13% vs. 5%); and the population of individuals that have completed secondary schooling was two-thirds of the observed share in the rest of Mexico (44% vs. 64%).

The distribution of the years of schooling does not tell the full story. It is also important to account for the quality of education. The World Bank's Human Capital Index provides a measure of learning-adjusted years of schooling to allow for assessing schooling quality in a given country as well as a cross-country comparison of education outcomes. Also, the World Bank's Education Statistics (EdStates) compiles comprehensive data for analysis of learning outcomes, among many other indicators on education access, expenditure by country, and more (World Bank, Education Statistics | Learning Outcomes,).

---

[3] These figures come from the 2010 Population Census.

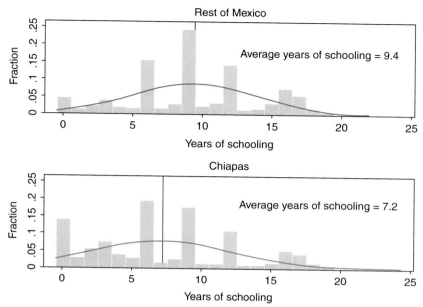

Figure 3 Years of schooling of the labor force: Chiapas versus rest of Mexico
Note: This figure was originally published in Hausmann, Espinoza, and Santos (2015). Copyright 2015 Hausmann, Ricardo; Espinoza, Luis; and Santos, Miguel Angel; and the President and Fellows of Harvard College. Permission for reprinting was obtained from M. A. Santos.
Source: 2010 Population Census

For many countries, the Program for International Student Assessment scores (PISA scores) of the OECD are available, providing students' standardized tests scores in the following topics: reading, mathematics, science, and other skills (PISA). For Latin American countries, UNESCO has conducted educational quality assessments called Second Regional Comparative and Explanatory Study (Valdés *et al.*, 2008) and Third Regional Comparative and Explanatory Study (Pizarro *et al.*, 2016). Additionally, country-specific standardized student assessments may be available, revealing differences at the sub-national level.

Data on educational assessments are useful to adjust for differences in the quality of schooling across countries and sub-national regions but should be interpreted with care. First, there may be implicit biases stemming from the way in which the tests have been deployed, whether they cover rural and poorer communities, which may be prone to suffer from lower quality of education. Second, recent assessments only reflect the current quality of education rather than the quality of education received by the current labor force. Third, test results are endogenous to several household characteristics, such as household income or the level of schooling of the head of household.

Going back to our Chiapas example, the Ministry of Education of Mexico runs the National Evaluation of Academic Achievement in School Establishments (ENLACE),[4] a standardized test held for all public and private schools at all pre-college levels measuring math and Spanish-language proficiency.[5] ENLACE test scores can be used to factor in the analysis differences in the quality of schooling, after correcting for the impact of some household characteristics that might be endogenous to the test results. In the case of Chiapas, quality results at the municipal level can be regressed against the maximum level of schooling in the household (other than the student), household income, and ethnicity. We then use the residuals between the actual test scores and test scores predicted based on the observed variables as our net indicator of education quality. The result is a corrected quality indicator that nets out the correlations between quality and a group of relevant variables.[6]

The results of both the unconditional and conditional performance for all Mexican states are presented – for Spanish and mathematics – in Figure 4. Differences between the quality of education as measured by the conditional or unconditional test indicator do not alter the existing skill spectrum of a particular place – poor results signal potential skill shortages, regardless of the origin – but they are relevant to the type of policy intervention that is needed to address the constraint. Chiapas' relative positioning in Spanish (panel a) does not change much between the unconditional (fourth from bottom) and conditional (third from bottom). When it comes to mathematics (panel b), the picture is somewhat different, as the state ranks third from bottom in the unconditional figure (just above Oaxaca and Guerrero, two Mexican states with significant indigenous population) but registers a moderate improvement when we control for relevant household characteristics (sixth from bottom).

Low levels of schooling and learning may signal potential constraints in human capital but are far from sufficient. As it turns out, these results might also be driven by the low demand for skills, which in turn reduces the incentives of individuals to invest in education. The key lies in having a robust analytical framework that allows us to tell these two situations apart.

---

[4] ENLACE is the Spanish acronym for *Evaluación Nacional de Logros Académicos en Centros Escolares.*

[5] Levels of schooling covered by the ENLACE test: primary (the last four grades), secondary (the three grades), and media superior (last grade).

[6] See Appendix 2 for estimating the quality of schooling.

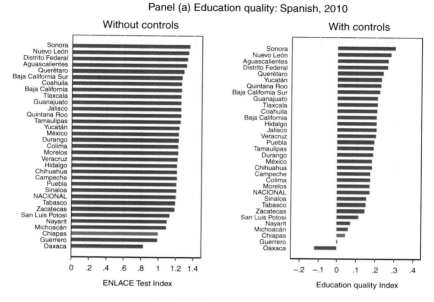

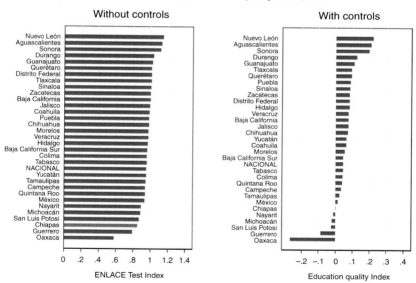

Figure 4 ENLACE assessment of educational quality by state

Note: This figure was originally published in Hausmann, Espinoza, and Santos (2015). Copyright 2015 Hausmann, Ricardo; Espinoza, Luis; and Santos, Miguel Angel; and the President and Fellows of Harvard College. Permission for reprinting was obtained from M. A. Santos.

Source: Minister of Education (ENLACE) and 2010 Population Census

2.1 The Shadow Price of Human Capital Should Be High

If an input is relatively scarcer than others, agents should be willing to pay a premium for it. That is the premise of the first principle of differential diagnosis. The labor force contributes varying levels of skills to the transformative process of producing goods and services. Additionally, among high-skilled labor, vast specializations exist at different relative prices. If one or more skills are a binding constraint to growth, the price differentials of these skills shall reflect their relative scarcity and be priced at a premium.

How can an analyst observe the skill premium? The main challenge in the deployment of this principle is the determination of the factor's price. Sometimes, production factors have observable market prices, such as the real interest rate in the case of financing or electricity tariffs in the case of the power sector. Yet, even considering these same factors, there are times when market distortions – credit rationing or interest rate ceilings in the case of finance and subsidized tariffs or power outages in the case of electricity – result in observed prices that are meaningless from an economic standpoint, as they do not reflect real relative scarcities. These distortions open a wedge between observed factor prices and the real cost of sourcing these factors for businesses. In those cases, we shall resort to shadow prices, which are estimated prices for factors for which no relevant market price exists.

In order to assess the relative scarcity of human capital in a specific place, we need to rely on shadow prices: the information required to arrive at the price businesses are willing to pay for skills is not readily available in most cases and requires some statistical processing.

Mincer Regressions

The method most widely used in economics to estimate the shadow price of skills is Mincer regression (Mincer, 1958). The typical Mincer regression estimates the monetary returns associated with an additional year of schooling, by modeling employment earnings as a function of years of schooling and experience.

$$Log\_income_i = \alpha + \beta_1 * years\ of\ schooling_i$$
$$+ \beta_2 * years\ of\ experience_i + \mu_i$$

By representing the individual's income derived from work in logarithms, Mincer regressions provide an easy interpretation of the coefficient of interest β_1: percentage increase in wages associated with an additional year of schooling. The model is flexible, allowing researchers to include other variables that might have a significant influence on wages in particular contexts, such as gender, ethnic origins, or foreign workers. It also allows to estimate the impact of different levels of education, by substituting years of schooling for discrete levels of completion such as primary, secondary, and tertiary education. Although Mincer regressions are mostly used to measure private returns to schooling and guide individual decisions on how much to invest in human capital, they also provide evidence on the relative scarcity of talent at different levels of schooling, experience, occupation, and other segments of the labor market.

Previous research based on Mincer regression reports that the distribution of Mincer returns tends to be centered on an average ranging between 5 and 8 percent per year of schooling, with fat tails ranging from 1 to 20 percent. Among the most recent research, highest returns to schooling are reported for women in sub–Saharan Africa (15 percent), whereas the lowest are for men in the Middle East and North Africa (6 percent). At a worldwide level, the highest returns accrue to tertiary education, followed by primary and then secondary schooling (Patrinos, 2016; Psacharopoulos and Patrinos, 2018).

Mincer regressions have their limitations, which have become more salient as rapid technological progress underscores the difference between actual skills and schooling (Heckman, Lochner, and Todd, 2003). The result of a Mincer regression is an average marginal rate of return for each additional year of schooling, yet the rate of return most likely varies in a nonlinear fashion as the number of years of schooling increases and potentially decreases over the working life cycle. Also, the model does not differentiate the quality or relevance of work experience, as the latter is usually defined as age minus years of schooling minus six (the typical school starting age). Mincer regressions only consider the opportunity cost of foregone wages. They do not account for taxes or benefits – which vary significantly by level of wages – or tuition costs. Despite that, they continue to serve as a good initial estimate of the return on schooling.

Modeling Mincer regressions normally requires hourly wage data. In many cases, particularly in developing countries, population census and labor force surveys report annual or monthly wages. Estimates of the returns to schooling using monthly or annual data can potentially be a better estimate of returns, as individuals with higher levels of schooling tend to work more hours for their wage (Card, 1999).

For a Mincer regression, we also need data sets at the worker level with wages, years of schooling, gender, and date and place of birth. If you are interested in testing if the skills of internal (within country) or external migrants are priced at a premium or at a discount, an additional field on place of work (to contrast with place of birth) will be needed. Typically, this information can be found in population or economic censuses, or labor force surveys. In most countries, these surveys include additional information that allows for controlling for observed individual characteristics (gender, ethnicity, and native language), work-specific characteristics (occupation and economic sector), and place-specific characteristics (urban or rural setting, indicators of know-how agglomeration).

Figure 5 portrays an example of the output of a Mincer regression to estimate the differential level of wages associated with different years of schooling in Mexico and the state Chiapas (Mexico's poorest state).[7] In estimating Mexico's Mincer coefficient, we can also control for place of origin, gender, and indigenous language (as a proxy for ethnic origins).[8,9] In order to estimate the average change in monthly wage associated with each year of schooling, the authors used the averages of each regressor per particular year.

For all levels of education, the wages of Mexican workers are significantly higher than those in Chiapas. On average, Chiapas' workers make 35.8 percent less than workers elsewhere in Mexico with the same level of schooling, experience, gender, and ethnic origin. An alternative reading of Figure 5 is

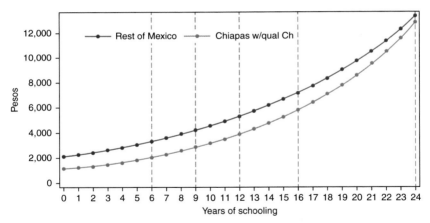

Figure 5 Returns to schooling in Chiapas versus the rest of Mexico
Note: This figure was originally published in Hausmann, Pietrobelli, and Santos (2021). Copyright 2021 Elsevier Inc. Permission for reprinting was obtained from M. A. Santos.
Source: 10 percent Microdata sample of 2010 Population Census (National Institute of Statistics and Geography [INEGI])

---

[7] The data come from the 10 percent microdata sample of the 2010 Population Census carried out by the National Institute of Statistics and Geography of Mexico (INEGI).
[8] See the specification and complete output of the Mincer regression in Appendix 1.
[9] Hausmann, Pietrobelli, and Santos (2021).

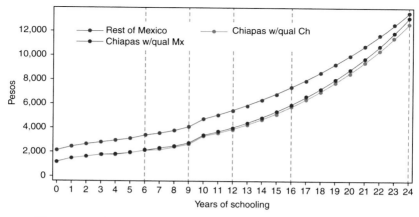

Figure 6 Differences in the quality of schooling between Chiapas
and the rest of Mexico

Note: This figure was originally published in Hausmann, Espinoza, and Santos (2015). Copyright 2015 Hausmann, Ricardo; Espinoza, Luis; and Santos, Miguel Angel; and the President and Fellows of Harvard College. Permission for reprinting was obtained from M. A. Santos.

Source: 10 percent Microdata sample of 2010 Population Census (INEGI)

that workers in Chiapas need twelve years of schooling to earn the same wage as workers elsewhere in Mexico with an average of six years of schooling.

One potential explanation behind different returns to schooling is differences in the quality of education. Based on the results reported by ENLACE and the correction for households' characteristics mentioned before, it is possible to reproduce the schedule of the expected value of wages by the level of education portrayed in Figure 5, by attributing to Chiapas' workers the average quality of education at each level of schooling in the rest of Mexico. The results are reported in Figure 6.

These results suggest that the difference in the quality of education between Chiapas and the rest of Mexico does not explain the large differences in wages at each level of schooling. Even after assigning to workers in Chiapas Mexico's average quality of education, the expected wage at each schooling level (the blue line in Figure 6) is still below the rest of Mexico (green) for workers with similar schooling, experience, gender, and indigenous origins.[10]

---

[10] Appendix 2 explains the methodology behind the estimation portrayed in Figure 6. Quality differences between Chiapas and the rest of Mexico at a high school level were assumed for college and above.

Mincer returns may provide additional insights when contrasted with unemployment figures. Low returns on tertiary schooling in the context of high unemployment of individuals with college degrees may signal an excess supply of skills relative to demand. Alternatively, a high return to tertiary schooling when unemployment among college degree holders is low, points toward an insufficient supply of skills in the economy. Similarly, high returns on tertiary schooling, coupled with high unemployment among individuals with no college degree, signal there is demand for high skills and firms' willingness to pay for them but also point out to a potential bottleneck preventing individuals from pursuing higher levels of education. Finally, high returns to tertiary schooling when unemployment among college degree holders is high may signal problems of quality of skills available (including quality of schooling or training) or misallocation of labor. Further analysis would be required to identify the drivers of the wage premium.

In cases where there is no microdata available to estimate returns to schooling, it is difficult to ascertain whether there is a premium on skills or not. Yet the analyst can observe the cost of labor through a variety of sources, which coupled with direct interviews with companies across the most relevant economic sectors can provide an initial assessment on the relative scarcity of skills. For example, ILOSTAT reports the hourly cost of labor for fifty-eight countries by economic activity.[11] Additionally, UNIDO compiles data sets on the manufacturing sector at a four-digit level in several countries, reporting sectoral output, wage bill, and the number of employees, among other variables.

The World Bank's Enterprise Survey may offer further insights into the scarcity of skills. We explore the experience of business establishments in Indonesia trying to hire employees across the skill spectrum, as reported by the 2015 Enterprise Survey. Figure 7 summarizes firms' responses when asked about obstacles to hiring: (1) managers and senior staff and (2) professionals and technicians. As portrayed by the red bar in both panels, 77.4 percent of establishments that tried to hire managers and senior professionals cited difficulty doing so due to the lack of the right skills; 64.7 percent for hiring high-skill technicians and professionals. This provides suggestive evidence that the supply of managerial and technical skills might be inadequate in Indonesia.

2.2 Changes in the Level of Human Capital Should Be Associated with Changes in Private Investment and Growth

If a factor is a binding constraint, improving its provision should lead to significant improvements in the objective function. More specifically, if

---

[11] Unfortunately, their database does not include low-income countries.

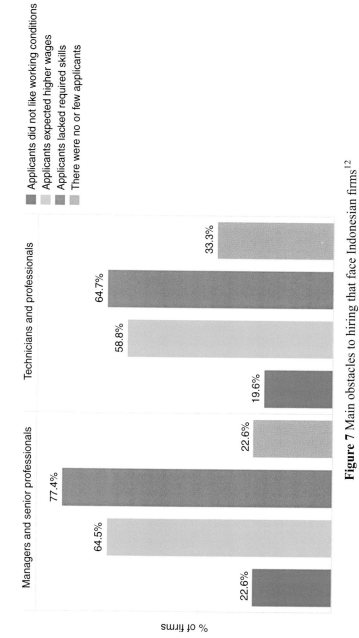

Figure 7 Main obstacles to hiring that face Indonesian firms[12]

Source: World Bank, Indonesia Enterprise Survey (2015)

---

[12] Percentages do not add to 100 percent because respondents can choose multiple obstacles.

human capital is constraining private investment, an increase in the availability of qualified labor should be accompanied by increased investments and growth (and vice versa).

Consider the contrasting cases of Ghana and Thailand. With the international drive to promote schooling, both countries embarked on large-scale programs to increase access to education, which led to the significant progress reported in the panel a) of Figure 8. As a matter of fact, Ghana was more successful, reversing the levels observed around 1965 and duplicating the average years of schooling of its workforce by 2010.

As reported in panel b) of Figure 8, the large increase in schooling in Ghana was not accompanied by a corresponding increase in GDP per capita, which stagnated over the following decades. In this case, it is hard to argue that lack of schooling or poor human capital was the most binding constraint to growth in Ghana. On the other hand, the somewhat slower – still impressive – improvement in schooling in Thailand was accompanied by a significant growth acceleration, in particular after 1990. This provides an initial indication that human capital might have been constraining economic growth in Thailand. As the constraint improved, there was an associated payoff in terms of investment and growth.

As persuasive as the panels in Figure 8 might be, they must be interpreted with care. After all, when an economy experiences a growth acceleration, there are usually multiple factors changing at the same time. This is particularly relevant when testing for human capital as a constraint, as changes tend to occur with a significant lag. Policies aimed at expanding access to education manifest in higher average years of schooling or higher quality of education in the labor force one or two decades down the road.

In the case of Thailand, the significant growth acceleration from 1990 onward is associated with a massive inflow of Japanese foreign direct investment (FDI) and know-how. At a critical time when Japanese firms were looking for countries with lower wages to build their plants, Thailand aggressively opened its economy and attracted a large number of these "flying geese" (Bernard and Ravenhill, 1995; Kojima, 2000; Kasahara, 2004). The improvement in schooling surely contributed to the readiness of the workforce, but the growth acceleration might not have occurred in the absence of the Japanese FDI boom.

Another interesting example from a sub-national context is again that of Chiapas. Over the twenty years following the Zapatista rebellion (1994), the federal government devoted significant attention and resources to the region, in an effort to address the large income gaps and prevent further social unrest (Hausmann, Pietrobelli, and Santos, 2021). One of the targets of public

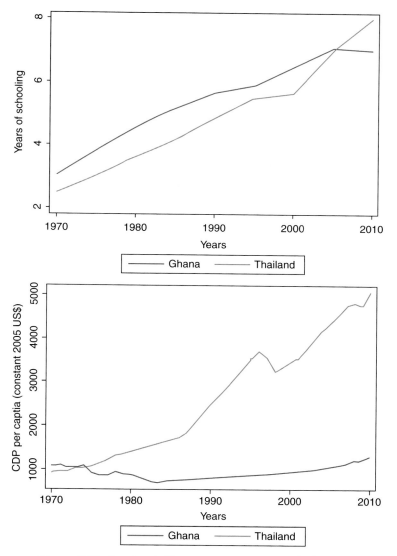

Figure 8 Thailand and Ghana: aggregate years of schooling
Source: Education Statistics (World Bank)

investment was reducing the schooling gap between Chiapas and the rest of Mexico. Figure 9 shows the schooling gap declined steadily, going from 3.2 years on average for the cohort born in 1965 to 2.2 years for those born in 1987.

And yet, the increase in schooling in Chiapas was not accompanied by a growth acceleration. In the twenty years between the Population Censuses

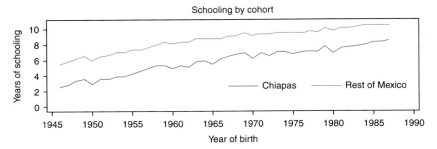

Figure 9 Schooling gap between Chiapas and rest of Mexico by year of birth
Note: This figure was originally published in Hausmann, Pietrobelli, and Santos (2018). Copyright 2018 Hausmann, Ricardo; Pietrobelli, Carlo; Santos, Miguel Angel; and the President and Fellows of Harvard College. Permission for reprinting was obtained from M. A. Santos.
Source: 2010 Population Census (INEGI)

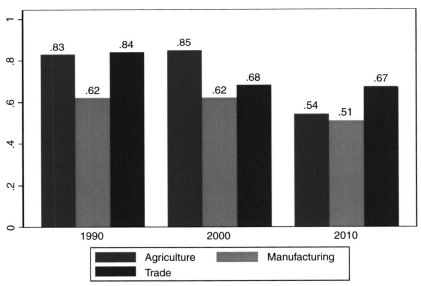

Figure 10 Relative wages by sector: Chiapas versus rest of Mexico
Note: This figure was originally published in Hausmann, Espinoza, and Santos (2015). Copyright 2015 Hausmann, Ricardo; Espinoza, Luis; and Santos, Miguel Angel; and the President and Fellows of Harvard College. Permission for reprinting was obtained from M. A. Santos.
Source: Mexican Population Census

of 1990 and 2010, the productivity gap between Chiapas' workers – as proxied by wages – and workers in the rest of Mexico widened. Figure 10 portrays the wages on the three most important sectors in the Chiapas' economy – representing on average two-thirds of all economic activity throughout the period – as a share of the average of workers in the rest of Mexico. In parallel to the rapid reduction in the schooling gap, relative wages in Chiapas fell 35 percent in agriculture, 20 percent in wholesale and retail, and 18 percent in manufacturing. This evolution provides suggestive evidence that human capital was not the main driver behind the large income gaps observed between Chiapas and the rest of Mexico.

In addition to improvements in schooling outcomes, other interventions that can lead to changes in the availability of human capital in a country include changes to immigration policies, the adoption of national or sectoral training programs, or new policies aimed at boosting the employability of the workforce, such as wage subsidies. Therefore, an analysis of the impact of such interventions at the sectoral or economy level on investment and growth can demonstrate whether "adding" skills to the economy translates into demand for these skills.

2.3 Agents Attempting to Overcome or Bypass Skill Shortages

When searching for potential binding constraints, it is important to remember that private companies must be well aware of the distortions holding them back and are likely working to overcome them. In the case of human capital, the efforts of agents attempting to bypass the constraint might be observed through several practices. For example, firms may be investing in resources or programs that allow them to increase access to skills, or they may be investing in training or retraining employees. How do their investments compare to investments made by firms in the same industry globally? Are firms attempting to hire skills outside the country? What about labor mobility between firms within the same sector? Is employee turnover (between firms) prevalent among skill-intensive sectors?

Enterprise Surveys: Obstacles Faced by Firms and Their Actions

It is possible to assess the extent to which skill shortages are constraining a country's growth prospects by analyzing the evolution of business practices coupled with the evolution of firms' complaints regarding production inputs. In doing so, it is useful to analyze both firms' indications of major obstacles to doing business, as well as the effort or cost or investments undertaken by firms to address the factor. Enterprise surveys are a useful source for these data.

Consider the case of Ecuador portrayed in Figure 11. The horizontal axis plots the share of firms offering formal training to their workers, whereas the vertical axis plots the share of firms that consider an *inadequately educated workforce* as one of the major obstacles in Ecuador. Green dots represent all countries worldwide for which the data required for both axes are available; orange dots represent a group of Ecuador's benchmark countries. Blue dots allow assessing the evolution of the relative positioning of Ecuador along these axes for available enterprise surveys (Enterprise Surveys Indicators Data).

According to Figure 11, by 2017 74 percent of firms in Ecuador offered formal training to their workers. This is the third-highest percentage in the world and the highest percentage among Latin American peers. Moreover, the number of firms offering formal training has increased steadily since 2006, a potential indicator that businesses are facing obstacles in finding the skills they need in the market and are therefore forced to invest in employee training.

Is this sufficient evidence to identify human capital as a potential constraint? The relative positioning of Ecuador along the vertical axis indicates that less than 5 percent of the firms surveyed consider an *inadequately educated workforce* as a major obstacle in Ecuador. This percentage is the lowest among Latin American peers. If we use business complaints as the shadow price of a potentially inadequately trained workforce, we can conclude that there may

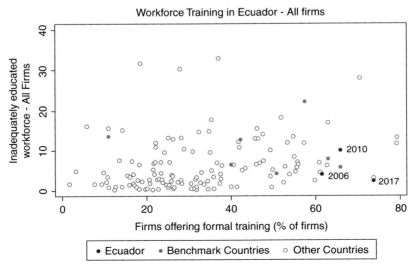

Figure 11 Ecuador: Firms offering formal training versus labor force inadequacy

be other more important obstacles constraining productivity and growth in Ecuador.

Now consider the case of Chile (Figure 12). Despite having a lower number of firms offering formal training (58 percent), by 2010, 22 percent of the business surveyed considered an *inadequately educated workforce* to be their number one obstacle. This is the highest percentage among Latin American peers – twice the share of the first runner-up – suggesting businesses incur significant costs (shadow price) to secure the skills they need. As a matter of fact, together with labor regulations (24 percent), these are the two most significant hurdles identified by firms surveyed in Chile.[13]

The analysis previously described can be used to assess whether human capital is a potential constraint to firms of different types: based on size (small, medium, or large), sector (manufacturing or services), the origin of capital (domestic or foreign), and tradability of output (exporting or non-exporting).

Migrant Wage Premium

Firms may also attempt to bypass skill shortages by importing labor – a dynamic of which Panama is a prime example. Between 2005 and 2015, Panama earned its place among the top-ten fastest-growing economies in the world. Contrary to

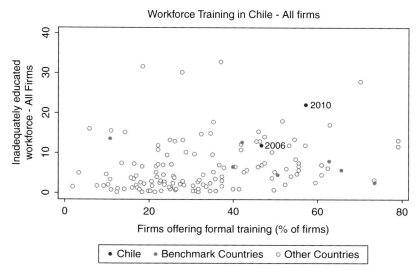

Figure 12 Chile: firms offering formal training versus labor force inadequacy

the patterns observed in most developing countries, the export-led boom relied exclusively on services. Exports of transportation and logistics, business services, and travel receipts coming from the air hub at Tocumen Airport quadrupled, paving the way for Panama to double its income per capita within a decade (Hausmann, Obach, and Santos, 2016).

Service sectors are skill-intensive. In order to increase the supply of skills, Panama relied on two policy devices. First, in 2006 Congress passed Law 41, a bill granting companies that establish their headquarters in Panama a complete tax holiday and various regulatory benefits, including unrestricted work visas for their employees. One year later, a massive industrial park – Panama Pacific – was created on the premises of a former US military base. Within that special economic zone, firms got certain tax benefits, including an allowance to hire foreign workers beyond the 10 percent cap imposed by Panama's labor regulation. Ten years down the road, 117 multinational companies had established their headquarters in Panama, and 251 firms had joined Panama Pacific. These policies eased the supply of know-how required by high-skill tradable services to flourish. The ensuing growth acceleration suggests that human capital might have been the most binding constraint to investment and growth in Panama in the early 2000s, but ten years of rapid growth seem to have dried out talent once again, in particular for firms operating outside the special economic zones.

Figure 13 describes the premiums earned by foreign workers when compared with Panamanians, as estimated by a Mincer regression controlling for schooling, years of experience, gender, ethnicity, occupation (panel a), and industry (panel b).[14] According to the latest Population Census, by 2010, foreign workers earned on average a wage premium of 47 percent over comparable Panamanians. All premiums to foreign workers were positive and statistically significant across the spectrum of industries and occupations. Within industries, the highest wage premium for foreigners (72 percent) was recorded by one of the industries that led the growth acceleration: transportation and storage. Within professions, foreign managers earned a premium of 70 percent over similar Panamanians; 54 percent in the case of professionals, scientists, and intellectuals; and 53 percent for services and sales.

A few insights can be derived from Figure 13. First, businesses in Panama overcame skill shortages and human capital constraints by hiring foreign talent. Second, while lifting restrictions to foreign workers relaxed the constraint and enabled a rapid growth acceleration in Panama, there is significant evidence

---

[14] Wage premiums are estimated by a Mincer regression controlling for education, experience, gender, and ethnicity, with occupation (panel a) and industry fixed effects (panel b). Estimates and 95 percent confidence interval are shown. See Appendix 3 for a more detailed description of the specification used.

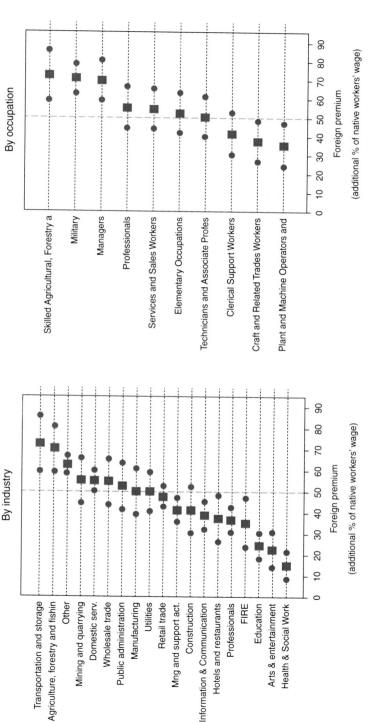

Figure 13 Panama: foreign wage premium by industry and occupation

Note: This figure was originally published in Hausmann, Ricardo; Obach, Juan; Santos, Miguel Angel; and the President and Fellows of Harvard College. Permission for reprinting was obtained from M. A. Santos. **Source:** Population Census 2010 (INEC)

indicating that by 2010, skills brought by foreign workers were again in short supply and businesses were willing to pay dearly for them. Most businesses in Panama complained about the high turnover rates driven by aggressive competition for the available talent (Hausmann, Obach, and Santos, 2016). That same year (2010), the share of businesses in Panama identifying the need to invest in *retraining workforce* came only second (to corruption) in the World Bank's Enterprise Survey.

These results suggest that foreign workers brought skills that were not available in the Panamanian economy, and therefore came to complement those supplied by domestic workers. Otherwise, it would be very hard to explain why businesses in tradable sectors would be willing to pay such high premiums for foreign talent. Yet the case of Panama – positive and statistically significant wage premiums for foreigners across all industries and occupations – is unique.

Consider now the case of Jordan, which witnessed a massive wave of refugee influx following the Syrian civil war (2011) and Arab Spring more broadly, resulting in a population increase of 50 percent between 2008 and 2017. Immigrants brought a varied array of skills, which were highly segmented by the country of origin. Within that context, an analysis of wage premiums to migrants from different countries by occupation provides a more nuanced understanding of the substitutability or complementarity of foreigners and their impact on the labor supply. Figure 14 portrays an estimation of wage premiums earned by foreign professionals (panel a) and technicians and associate professionals (panel b) by country of origin (Hausmann *et al.*, 2019).[15]

For professionals, Syrian immigrants earned significantly lower wages than their Jordanian counterparts. This feature is in stark contrast with immigrants coming from non–Arab countries, for whom the wage premiums were positive, significant, and large. These results suggest that non–Arab professionals brought valuable skills that were scarce within the Jordanian labor market, and businesses were willing to pay a premium for them. When it comes to technicians and associate professionals, non–Arab immigrants do not seem to earn significantly more or less than their Jordanian counterparts, but there is a large positive wage premium for Arabs coming from other countries. This pattern suggests that some immigrants provide unique know-how and skills that complement that of Jordanian workers.

Firms might attempt to overcome human capital constraints by investing large sums in retraining workers or bringing in foreign labor with the know-how that are scarce in the domestic market. In this situation, restrictions to hire

---

[15] Wage premiums are calculated through a Mincer regression that controls for education, experience, gender, and industry fixed effects. Estimates and 95 percent confidence interval are shown.

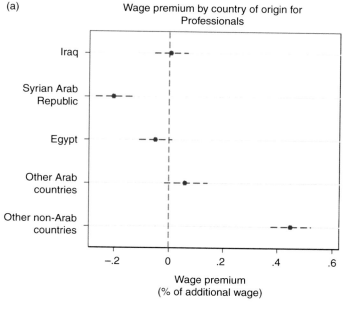

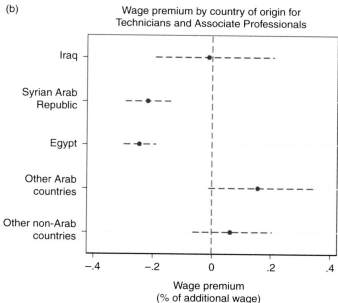

Figure 14 Jordan: wage premiums to foreigners, selected occupations (2016)
Source: CID calculations based on Harmonized Labor Force Surveys (HLFS 2016)
(OAMDI, 2017)

foreign workers with skills that are complementary to those of domestic workers usually result in businesses competing for talent and driving wage premiums
upward, which in turn might discourage further investment and affect the
competitiveness of companies operating in tradable industries.[16]

2.4 Camels and Hippos: Agents Less Intensive in Human Capital Are More Likely to Thrive (and Vice Versa)

The premise of the fourth test is that the business footprint of an economy –
what is present and what is not – is informative of its most binding constraints. It
relies on a metaphor first introduced by Hausmann, Klinger, and Wagner
(2008): What we observe in a place is indicative of what factors are in relative
abundance and which ones are relatively scarcer. More specifically, the fact that
the animals we tend to observe and thrive in a desert are not intensive in water
(such as camels) and that others that are absent tend to be more water-intensive
(such as hippos), suggests that the supply of water might be a binding constraint
in those places.

If a factor is binding, firms in sectors that rely on that factor more intensely
are expected to be relatively less prevalent in the economy. At the same time,
firms that are less intensive in the use of this factor are expected to thrive.
Another way to think about this principle is that if a factor is binding, we would
expect to see firms moving away from industries or products that rely more on
the factor as an input to production, toward industries or products that are less
dependent on that particular factor. In the case where human capital is a binding
constraint, we would expect to see firms moving away from skill-intensive
industries – that is, sophisticated industries that require more skills – toward
capital-intensive industries.

Nunn (2007) offers a method to test if a country's exports are more or less
dependent on country-specific factors. Although this contribution was originally
aimed at assessing the impacts of contract intensiveness on exports, we can use
the same principles to test the marginal impact of country-specific factors on
economic activity. To quantify these impacts, Nunn (2007) models a country's
exports by sector as an interaction between the country's characteristics or factors
and the sector's dependency on these factors. For example, a sector that is skill-
intensive in a country with an adequate skills supply will contribute relatively
more to the country's exports. Alternatively, a sector that is skill-intensive in

---

[16] The regressions estimating these premiums are imperfect. Despite controlling for observed traits,
there will likely remain unobserved traits that partially explain wage premiums. As such, it is
crucial to complement these analyses with interviews with businesses in sectors registering the
more extreme premiums.

a country with a skills shortage will contribute relatively less to the country's exports.

South Africa stands in a showcase for this test. For decades, apartheid excluded and impoverished Black South Africans, restricting them to second-class education while at the same time subsidizing the use of capital. As a result, the only employment options for most Black South Africans were located far from urban centers, either in unskilled agriculture or in mining (Levinsohn, 2008).

Since the transition in 1994, reversing the legacy of economic exclusion has been at the center of policy and has proven to be a hard task (World Bank Group, 2018). Twenty-five years later, the unemployment rate in South Africa reached 28 percent (2019), with youth unemployment at twice that rate (56 percent). Additionally, unemployment has been persistent and pervasive among less skilled and less experienced workers, while wage and employment growth for skilled workers have increased. This begs the question of whether human capital is a binding constraint to private investments and subsequently to growth in South Africa, particularly given the historic exclusion and its legacy weighing down on the employability of its large Black majority. To answer this question, we examine the skill intensity of South Africa's exporting firms. Figure 15 provides an initial illustration of the relationship between South Africa's exports and skill intensity (top panel) and capital intensity (bottom panel). The downward (upward) trend between an industry's exports volume and skill (capital) intensity suggests that higher exports are associated with lower skill (higher capital) intensity.

We adapt Nunn's (2007) method to model the relationship between a country's exports and its industries' dependence on factors.[17] A positive relationship between industries' dependence on skills and the country's exports suggests that industries intensive in human capital are thriving and contribute more to the country's exports. On the other hand, a negative relationship between exports and industries' skill dependence variable indicates that industries intensive in the factor under study contribute less to country exports and hence may be struggling to grow.

To perform this analysis, a country's cross-sectional economic sector (or product) level data on trade flows need to be merged with the country's factor endowment (at least human capital and physical capital, but also other factors of interest for the study), and data on factor intensity by economic

---

[17] This can be done through a simple regression of a country's product exports on country factors and collecting the regression coefficients. This is demonstrated in Appendix 4.

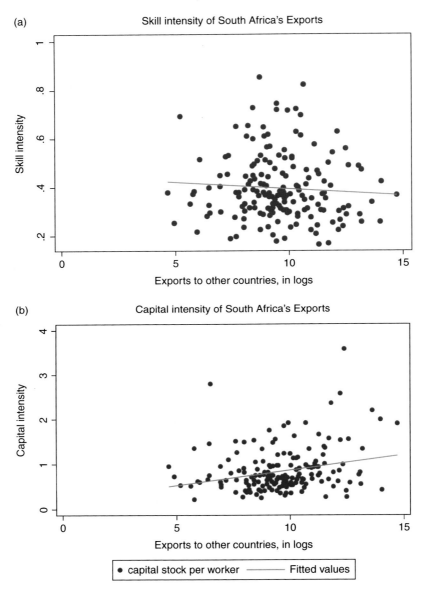

Figure 15 South Africa's product exports: factor intensity versus level of exports
Source: Own calculation using Nunn (2007) database

sector. Data on a country's factor endowment are often published – common sources include Hall and Jones (1999) and Antweiler and Trefler (2002).[18]

---

[18] We used Hall and Jones' (1999) estimate of physical and human capital for both panels of Figure 16.

The World Bank's human capital index (Angrist *et al.*, 2019) measuring learning outcomes can be useful to adjust human capital endowment measures, which are normally based on years of schooling. The most recent version of the Penn World Tables also has a human capital index. Data on industries' physical and human capital intensity are published by Bartelsman and Gray (1996), and Nunn (2007) and Rajan and Zingales (1998) who published sectoral contract- and financial-intensity measures, respectively. The sectoral intensity in other factors of interest may need to be constructed.

Figure 16 (top panel) shows the result of this analysis for South Africa and a group of chosen peers. The contribution of a country's skill-intensive industries to its exports is plotted on the horizontal axis. South Africa has a higher human capital stock than Brazil, Colombia, Mexico, and Indonesia (Hall and Jones, 1999), but the contributions of skill-intensive industries to exports are lower than in Colombia, Mexico, and Indonesia. Additionally, while the contributions of skill-intensive industries in these countries do not appear to be statistically different from zero, the contribution in South Africa is negative and statistically significant.

The bottom panel of Figure 16 models the relationship between countries' exports and industries' physical capital intensity. The contribution of capital-intensive industries to countries' exports is plotted on the horizontal axis. Similar to the top panel, a positive contribution implies industries with higher capital intensity are associated with a larger share of a country's export basket, and a negative contribution implies industries with higher capital intensity are associated with a lower share in a country's export basket. The result indicates that despite having a physical capital stock below that of Brazil, Chile, and Mexico (Hall and Jones, 1999), the contribution of South Africa's capital-intensive sectors to exports is higher – note that while the contribution of capital-intensive industries in Chile is larger in magnitude than in South Africa, the contribution is not statistically different from zero.

The lower prevalence of skill-intensive firms in exports, coupled with high youth unemployment as well as positive wage premiums and high employment for skilled workers (World Bank Group, 2018), supports the hypothesis that human capital is potentially a binding constraint in South Africa. The fact that these trends coexist with high unemployment rates among college graduates or educated youth suggests that the skills businesses are willing to pay high premiums for are not being acquired through the formal education system. As a matter of fact, the World Bank's human capital index (2020) reveals that despite receiving an average of ten years of schooling, these ten years are

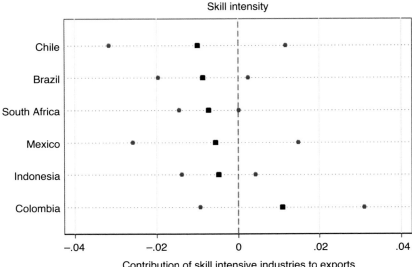

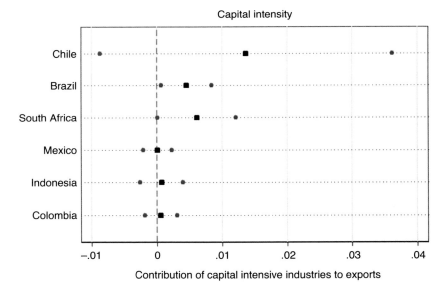

Figure 16 South Africa and benchmark countries: contribution of
factor-intensive industries to country's exports

Note: A contribution coefficient is statistically significant if the confidence
interval does not cross the zero line.

Source: Own calculation using Nunn (2007) database

equivalent to five years of schooling only – after adjusting for learning outcomes.[19]

These results are consistent with the empirical evidence reported in the economic literature. Subramanian and Alleyne (2001) documented that in spite of its comparative advantage in labor-intensive activity, South Africa is a net exporter of capital-intensive goods. The authors conclude that South African firms continue to favor physical capital over human capital and present a hypothesis of a malfunctioning labor market, where the cost of labor is high relative to the cost of capital. Levinsohn (2008) argues that structural deficiencies keep South African labor unemployable and proposes wage subsidies to lower the cost of labor as well as import skills through immigration. Lastly, Banerjee *et al.* (2008) offer a variety of hypotheses to explain the unemployability of South African labor, ranging from malfunctioning of labor market institutions that hinder the possibilities of the Black majority to participating in the labor force to a mismatch in supply and demand of skills.

3 From Diagnostic Symptoms to the Syndrome and Therapeutics

In Section 2, we demonstrate the deployment of the four diagnostic principles to test for human capital as a binding constraint to growth. This is the first of five steps of the Growth Diagnostic process (Figure 17) and enables to identify any symptoms that point toward human capital being binding. Next, based on the evidence revealed through the diagnostic signals, an analyst shall pose a hypothesis explaining the equilibrium state in the country and how human capital is binding (step 2) proving or disproving that policy interventions targeting human capital (stock or allocation) will indeed have the highest impact on investment or growth rates (step 3), compared to other potential constraints (step 4). Only then can the analyst proceed to therapeutics – or elements of public policy to address human capital constraints present in an economy (step 5).

3.1 The Syndrome: Why Does This Equilibrium Persist?

Establishing human capital as a binding constraint requires formulating a hypothesis based on the deployment of the diagnostic signals, explaining (1) the mechanism by which human capital is effectively constraining investment and growth and (2) why this equilibrium persists. We call this hypothesis

---

[19] Learning-adjusted years of schooling are defined for country C as the product of average years of schooling (s_c) and a measure of learning (international standardized test score) relative to the average score of the top-performing country (L_n, as per the World Bank 2020 Human Capital Index Update, Singapore).

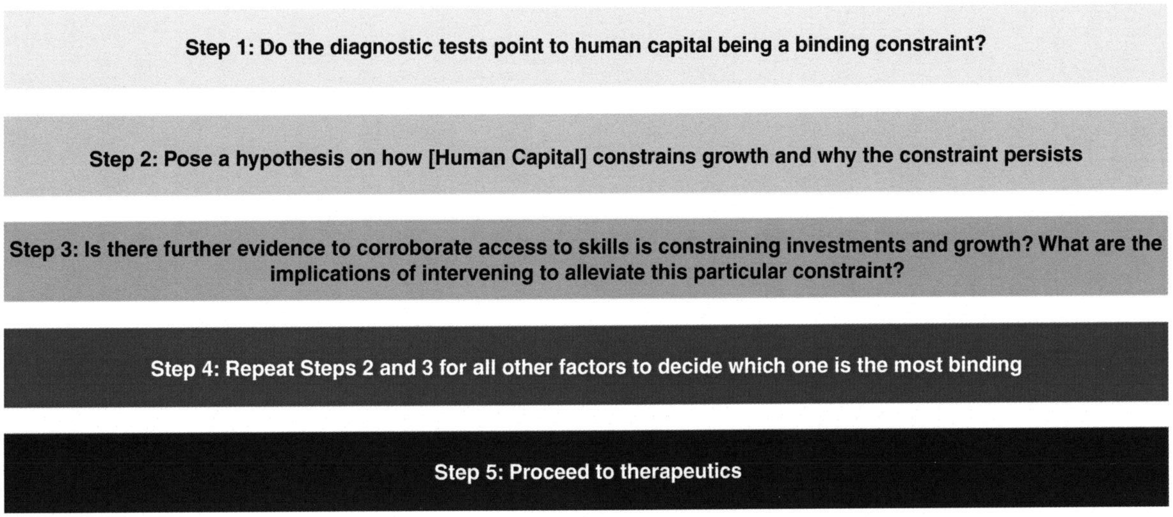

Step 1: Do the diagnostic tests point to human capital being a binding constraint?

Step 2: Pose a hypothesis on how [Human Capital] constrains growth and why the constraint persists

Step 3: Is there further evidence to corroborate access to skills is constraining investments and growth? What are the implications of intervening to alleviate this particular constraint?

Step 4: Repeat Steps 2 and 3 for all other factors to decide which one is the most binding

Step 5: Proceed to therapeutics

Figure 17 The Growth Diagnostic process

a syndrome. In the case where human capital is a binding constraint, the syndrome can start with one of two premises. First, the supply of skills is inadequate and does not meet the demand coming from existing firms. The second is that firms are unable to hire the workers or skills they need due to market failures leading to misallocation of skills (Figure 18). The diagnostic tests presented in Section 2 provide the evidence necessary to characterize the symptoms and shall be used as entry points to formulate a hypothesis on the state of human capital in the country.

Insufficient quantities of a skill: A combination of high Mincerian returns-in general or on one or more specific skills in particular-and high employment rates among individuals possessing those skills, in addition to foreign hiring or similar efforts by firms to increase their access to specific skills, may signal that human capital is a potential binding constraint. The high attrition of firm employees and their movement across competing firms are other signals of insufficient quantities of skills being a constraint. Alternatively, the skill short-age can be binding to an extent that it forces firms and available skills to migrate outside the country. In this case, an analyst can find a high Mincerian return on the skill in shortage yet with attrition as skills move abroad.

Low quality of available skills: If the quality of available skills – say, engineer-ing – is low, one can expect to see relatively higher unemployment rates among engineers (compared to the case where the quantity of engineers is binding). Yet stronger signals include large investments in training reported by firms. A situation of low quality of available skills could be mistaken for a problem of technological coordination failure, and vice versa. In several developing countries, degree holders – in this example, engineers – may be unable to work in their fields of specialization. Is this a signal of low quality of their skills, or rather the result of low demand? The hiring of foreign engineers may signal low quality of domestic skills while the emigration of domestic engineers or demand for their skills abroad may signal low demand for high skills in the country, and hence signals a technological coordination constraint rather than a human capital constraint.

In the case where certain firms lack access to the required skills due to misallocation, an analyst can expect to see the employment of skills in shortage concentrated in one or a few sectors, with little movement to firms in need of skills over the years. This situation can coexist with a premium on the skill in other sectors and even unemployment. For example, if individuals prefer to work in a specific sector an analyst can observe high unemployment of skilled individuals, due to distortions preventing the matching of existing skills to opportunities or jobs. In the meantime, firms may be willing to pay a premium on skills.

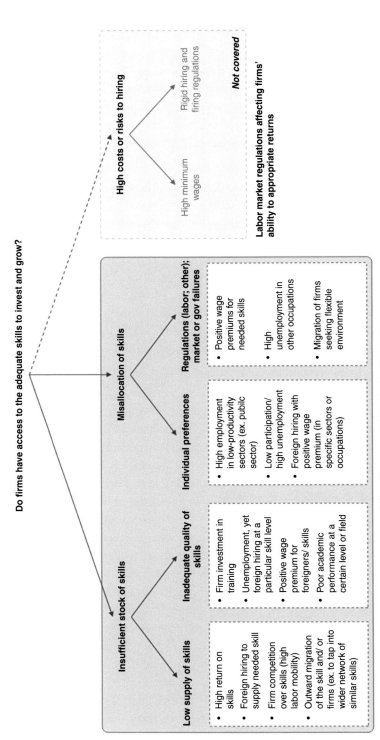

Figure 18 Evidence corresponding to a human capital constraint

3.2 Policy Options to Address Human Capital Constraints

If the analyst concludes that human capital is indeed a binding constraint to growth, the policy strategy to alleviate or release the constraint will depend on the hypothesis or syndrome. This section maps each of the previously mentioned hypotheses to several policies. It is important to note that this mapping is not a general recommendation of these specific policies to foster private investments and ultimately growth. Instead, the policy options discussed here should be embedded and contextualized in a more comprehensive strategy to foster investment and ignite economic growth in situations where human capital is indeed the most binding constraint.

The actual impact of the policies discussed in this section will depend almost exclusively on the country context – more specifically the administrative capabilities and political landscape. As such, a serious analysis of a bureaucracy's implementation capacity, its ability to coordinate with the private sector, and political space should guide the decision to adopt any policy and its implementation strategy (Pritchett, Samji, and Hammer, 2013). The process of selecting and implementing a course of action and monitoring its impact can help policy-makers capture nuanced information and knowledge about the human capital shortages facing the country and further improve the policy-making process.

Education Reform

The policy elements discussed in this section are short or medium-term solutions to address skill shortages within a specific country, especially as they may support youth employment by lowering the barriers to finding a first job through which new labor market entrants can then build experience and skills. This leaves out the question of reform of the education system. While we do not discuss education reform here, it is important to note that a country's long-term skills spectrum is dependent on its undertaking of education reform at the appropriate schooling levels to equip future generations with the needed skill set, hence effectively expanding the country's spectrum of skills. As a matter of fact, investments in the education system have the potential to preempt human capital constraints in the long run, by ensuring an adequate supply of skills as generations currently in schools begin to enter the labor market.

Yet education reform is not a pragmatic solution when human capital is constraining investment and growth in a place at present, as it cannot impact the country's skills spectrum in the present but rather promises augmented skills in the future. As such, alleviating human capital constraints will unlikely be achieved through education reform solely. This is not a reason to discard investments to improve the education system, but policy-makers ought to prepare for the future while making policy choices to support short-term growth.

3.2.1 Training Programs and Subsidies to Support Skills Formation

The most common intervention for country governments facing skill shortages has been supplying technical and vocational education and training (TVET). TVET often seeks to provide specific skills lacking in the economy that are required by existing firms, on the premise that workers lack these needed skills or are, for one reason or another, unable to acquire them (think of inability to seek education or training due to credit constraints). As such, governments have traditionally attempted to supply TVET by establishing national training programs or on-the-job training, to help would-be workers acquire the required skills. The latter could happen through a variety of mechanisms, such as subsidies, training taxes, levies, and so on.

The evidence for the effectiveness of such traditional policy interventions is limited. McKenzie (2017) surveyed an array of traditional labor market policies, including programs that provide TVET to the unemployed. He documented that training programs have a very modest impact on the employment of a country's workforce by firms. One possible explanation of this finding is that if firms do not hire workers due to skill gaps that impact their employability, training programs may in the short-term fill specific sets of skill gaps but are unlikely to change the long-run outlook in terms of skills availability. This is corroborated by South Korea's experience with TVET, where national (public) standards for training were not always able to meet demand.

Also, the drive to subsidize on-the-job training and require employers to train employees is often met with pushback and little take-up from employers. Again, South Korea's early experience with TVET – as well as South Africa's – shows the limitations of publicly subsidizing on-the-job training where firms often lack the incentive or interest in providing on-the-job training or are burdened by the often-complex implementation requirements (World Bank Group, 2018). This situation is often exacerbated if firms are unsure whether they can reap the benefit from their investment in employees if they are likely to exit and move to another job or firm once trained.

This does not mean training programs will never be effective, but rather emphasizes that the ultimate result depends on the program design and its suitability to the context of the country. South Korea is one example where industrialization implied an increase in the demand for specialized skills to an extent that trained workers were in shortage. For decades, South Korea experimented with and iterated the design of TVET programs to arrive at a suitable design. After attempting subsidized training, requiring on-the-job training, and offering publicly funded training, South Korea launched publicly funded training consortiums that leverage the country's large companies (such as Samsung, Hyundai, etc.) as well as universities to lead the training design by providing the curriculum, instructors, and material needed for the training. These consortiums have been successful in addressing skill gaps (Uh, 2018).

3.2.2 Immigration Policy

While addressing human capital constraints by means of improving the coverage and quality of education requires a long-term horizon, countries are still urged to grow, and firms still require skills to be able to carry on their economic activity at a competitive return on investment. Firms unable to meet their needs for specific skills and know-how in the domestic market may be able to overcome that constraint by means of foreign labor and sourcing talent abroad that complements local workers. This strategy has been pursued by many countries.

In such scenarios, immigrants can be relied on to supply the country with skills and perform activities that tend to be essential for firms' survival and proliferation, ultimately contributing to growth and job creation. If the skills required by firms to invest, innovate, and grow are lacking, the scope for innovation and growth is limited. As such, instead of innovating and introducing new products to the economy, firms would be limited to compete in sectors/products for which available skills are suited. That is the challenge often posed by the structural transformation process in developing countries. Firms with access to foreign talent are able to build up the capabilities needed to innovate; innovation leads to productive diversification and global competitiveness, thereby stimulating further investment and growth.

The main concern for policy-makers, when it comes to using immigration policy to attract the required skills, is whether foreigners would displace the local workforce. That would depend on the extent to which immigrants substitute or complement domestic workers across the skill spectrum. When immigrants bring complementary skills, they contribute to easing out the human capital constraint, thus allowing countries to grow and creating jobs for domestic workers that would not have been generated otherwise. We see evidence of the complementary of low and high-skilled immigrants in the case of Panama as immigrants experience positive wage premiums across occupations (see Section 2.4). Similarly, in 2017, one individual firm in

Jordan launched a software development branch and by mid-2018 employed around 100 high-skilled Jordanian software engineers. Due to restrictions on high-skilled migration, the firm initially struggled to hire just two foreign managers with the know-how and on-the-job experience on the firm's business model – a form of human capital lacking in Jordan. The absence of this experience would have hindered this significant investment that later generated jobs for 100 high-skilled Jordanians. Had this firm been unable to overcome the challenge, it would have most likely moved its investment to another country. In this particular case, the experience and skills provided by each of the two foreign workers were complementary to the talent of 50 Jordanians (Hausmann *et al.*, 2019).

3.2.3 Foreign Direct Investment

Similar to migration, FDI is another channel through which foreign know-how can be deployed to build up the domestic skills spectrum. While FDI by itself is not a channel used to introduce skills (rather, it is a channel for technology transfer), FDI can have positive spillovers, adding to the types and level of skills available in a country (Javorcik and Spatareanu, 2008).

   The case of Bangladesh's garment sector success is an example of how FDI can spur sector growth, primarily by infusing technical skills and know-how of the sector into the economy. Bangladesh's textile sector miracle started with a joint venture between a domestic firm, DESH, and Korean manufacturer, Daewoo. Rhee (1990) describes how 115 of the initial 130 Bangladeshi workers trained by Daewoo in Korea left DESH to set up, at different moments in time, their own garment-exporting firms. This transfer of skills from Daewoo to DESH employees was essential for the Bangladeshi economy to form a working population able to compete in and grow the garments sector in the country.

   To the extent that FDI brings in immigrants or transfers specialized skills allowing the relevant sectors to expand and grow, it is a channel to enhance a country's skills spectrum.

3.2.4 Wage Subsidies

An alternative view to active labor market policies to address skill gaps in the economy is helping them overcome excessive labor regulations and reduce the associated costs that are preventing them from hiring and developing talent. Within the context of this Element, we are only focused on labor market regulations that may hinder or restrict skill formation.

Policy-makers may find themselves in a situation where human capital constraints derive from the limited employability of certain population groups (typically, youth graduating from school and college), whose productivity or skill level is low relative to labor market wages (or minimum wages). For this population, securing employment is by itself an investment in their human capital, given the skills they build through learning by doing and on-the-job experience. In such a scenario, firms may be reluctant to hire these workers. Their reluctance will vary based on the cost of investing in the workers (through hiring and training) and the likelihood of appropriating the return on the investment. If the cost of this initial investment in hiring and investing in workers is high, firms may not accept the uncertainty about a worker's quality and productivity. Hiring the needed talent and further building their skills become a risky undertaking.

In such instances, when risks with regard to worker productivity or the cost of the initial investment are preventing firms from accessing would-be talent, wage subsidies and reduced regulations can help alleviate the issue. Wage subsidies would encourage firms to undertake this initial risky investment of hiring, and workers would be able to expand their skill set through learning by doing on the job (Levinsohn, 2008). In 1994, the government of Mexican President Ernesto Zedillo successfully convinced Japanese harness manufacturing Yazaki to open operation in Chiapas by offering wage subsidies over a training period of three months. That year, the first Yazaki plant opened in Tuxtla Gutierrez, Chiapas' capital, employing 600 domestic workers. Twenty years down the road, Yazaki had five production facilities in different municipalities of Chiapas and employed more than 3,000 workers (Hausmann, Pan, and Santos, 2020).

The drawbacks of wage subsidies are the possibility of rent-seeking and their potential to introduce direct or indirect distortions in the economy. Similar to the other policies we discuss in this section, country context and implementation capabilities will determine wage subsidies' success.

3.2.5 Other: Easing Labor Market Misallocations

The policy proposals previously mentioned might be helpful when the quantity or quality of available skills is insufficient. Yet there may be situations where human capital constraints are driven by market failures, where the extensive margin of labor supply does not respond to firm demand, leaving firms unable to locate and hire skills. Spatial and sectoral misallocations of labor are two scenarios to exemplify this problem. For example, if the working population at the managerial level displays a preference to work in the public sector or specific sectors, firms may be deprived of the required managerial skills. In these cases, policy interventions to correct the market failure can potentially alleviate the constraint.

The case of South Africa is one where sectors have favored the use of capital relative to labor following the historical and deliberate exclusion of Blacks. Specifically, Black South Africans were prevented from relocating closer to urban areas – the center of economic activity. Until the present day, the spatial patterns perpetuated by apartheid leave Blacks at the periphery of urban centers and pose a serious challenge to their ability to access employment opportunities (Levinsohn, 2008). Jordan's universally low female labor participation can be another example of a country where a large stock of highly qualified human capital is available but remains out of specific sectors or occupations because of a combination of cultural norms and labor regulations making it onerous for firms to hire and retain women (Kasoolu *et al.*, 2019).

McKenzie (2017) describes the sectoral and spatial misallocations of labor as the largest market failure in labor markets, as individual skills' may be located in one market but demanded in another. There are situations where certain groups experience high costs in entering the labor market or specific sectors within the economy. That effectively excludes them from participating, preventing firms that may be searching for those skills from accessing them. In these cases, policy-makers must consider interventions that are targeted to reducing the cost of entry of these groups into the labor market or specific sectors. These might include housing subsidies or investment in transportation systems to facilitate workers' mobility. Alternatively, governments can design incentives encouraging firms to relocate closer to workers (Banerjee *et al.*, 2008).

Conclusion

Investments in human capital should be expected to deliver growth dividends when other capabilities or inputs are not missing. We develop a framework based on the principles of Growth Diagnostics (Hausmann, Rodrik, and Velasco, 2008) and illustrate the deployment of four diagnostic signals to enable practitioners to test if human capital is indeed the most binding constraint and shall be a policy priority for a country's growth strategy.

The question of human capital as a binding constraint to growth is whether the skill spectrum in the country is sufficient for firms to engage in productive economic activities in a competitive way. In such situations, improvements in human capital are likely to lead to growth acceleration. The answer to this question is ultimately an empirical endeavor that seeks to understand country-specific factors and their underlying dynamics. Econometric analysis at the aggregate (national) level can tell us a lot about the dynamics of output and human capital; but assessing the adequacy of a country's specific need for human capital requires an observation of firm and worker behavior and decisions at a micro-level. Our framework relies on econometric analyses performed using what is usually the most granular data available for a country – population and economic censuses, household surveys, labor force surveys, and business surveys – but not amenable to comparisons across countries.

The nature of human capital makes the diagnostic exercise a real challenge. On the one hand, characterizing a country's human capital stock is difficult due to the varied and continuous nature of the skills spectrum. Contrary to other production factors such as electricity, water, finance, or infrastructure, human capital is not directly observable. On the other hand and perhaps even more problematic, a country's skill spectrum is highly heterogeneous, with different types and levels of skills easing or constraining different economic activities. Some of the examples we have provided documented cases where human capital was binding across industries and occupations, as signaled by the large wage premiums paid to foreigners and complaints about high turnover; But this is a rare occurrence. More often, the shortage of human capital is present in a specific set of occupations and constrains investment within a subset of industries that are more reliant on those skills. To navigate these complexities, we recommend a deductive approach, going from the more general definitions and aggregates to the more specific (at the industry or occupational level), and let the process be informed by a comprehensive set of interviews with decision-makers at the most relevant industries.

Not all diagnostic signals characterizing the most binding constraints can be unequivocally tested. A good rule is to rely on rigorous econometric analyses to test if the shadow price of a factor is high (the first diagnostic signal), or if more skill-intensive businesses tend to contribute less to value-added, employment, or exports (the fourth diagnostic signal). Other signals such as observing changes in policies affecting human capital and the corresponding changes in investment or growth (the second diagnostic signal) require delving through historical country data to pinpoint meaningful movements in human capital that could be referenced. Yet such changes need to be interpreted with care, as countries seldomly experience policy changes in a vacuum. Instead, they tend to occur alongside several other parallel fluctuations, and these relationships are prone to suffer from endogeneity and omitted variable biases that make it difficult to assert causality. Finally, in our experience, engaging in interviews with private actors and policy-makers is essential to capture the context and particularly useful in understanding agents' efforts to bypass the constraint (the third diagnostic signal). An exercise that is usually helpful when it comes to identifying these practices is to search for positive deviants in the country: businesses that we would not expect to be there – as they are very intensive in the use of the potential binding constraint – but have somehow figure out a way to get around it.

Growth Diagnostics are as much an art as a science. The framework provides a combination of rigorous quantitative methods, back-of-the-envelope calculations, and suggestions on where to look for anecdotal evidence. Policy practitioners shall assemble a variety of quantitative and qualitative evidence based on these methods and weigh the merits of the available evidence for each factor vis-à-vis alternative production inputs. Judging whether human capital is the most binding constraint can only be made by the analyst once the evidence available on all production inputs has been considered.

If there is significant evidence pointing out to shortages of human capital as the most binding constraint in the economy, we need a policy response with the potential to yield results in the short term. Accordingly, our toolkit focuses on policies that rely on public–private coordination to address shortages of the human capital of different nature, either due to insufficient skills (training programs or subsidies to support skill formation, a dynamic immigration policy to facilitate the import of missing skills, fostering FDI) or misallocation of existing skills (wage subsidies to compensate hefty labor regulations, or active policies to ease misallocations of resources in the labor market).

Pursuing our goal of providing a practical analytical framework for policy practitioners to assess whether human capital is indeed the most binding constraint has come at the price of two important limitations. First, in our diagnostic tree, we have separated for analytical purposes two different drivers of human capital shortages: insufficient skills and distortions or misallocations driven by labor regulations or cultural norms. In doing so, we have assumed that you can test for one isolating from the other, as well as independently from labor market regulations, when in fact these are potentially related and reinforce each other. Second, the very nature of the tests and underlying data allows the analyst to determine if human capital is constraining investment for existing business (the intensive margin) but is not directly informative on whether human capital is constraining the advent of new industries (the extensive margin). Productive diversification to drive economic growth entails sorting a chicken-and-egg dilemma: new industries might be missing because the place lacks the skill spectrum required, which in turn will not develop as long as these industries are missing. Thus, the policy toolkit we have outlined will likely apply to situations where insufficient skills are constraining the appearance of new economic activities, but the process of determining if human capital is indeed the most binding constraint to productive diversification will likely require further refinement.

Appendix 1

Mincer Regression for Mexico and Chiapas

A Tobit model or a censored regression model is used to estimate the relationship between income and years of schooling, modeled according to equation (1). The purpose is to estimate the returns on an additional year of schooling in Chiapas versus the rest of Mexico.

$$Log\_income = \alpha + \beta_1 * years\ of\ schooling + \beta_2 * years\ of\ experience$$
$$+\beta_3 * (years\ of\ experience)^2 + \beta_4 * female$$
$$+\beta_5 * (indigenous\ language) + \beta_6 * Chiapas, \qquad Equation(1)$$

- *Female* – a dummy variable for gender: 0 – male and 1 – female
- *Indigenous language* – a dummy variable for speaking an indigenous language (a proxy for ethnic origin): 0 – does not speak an indigenous language and 1 – speaks an indigenous language
- *Chiapas* – a dummy variable for the state: 0 – rest of Mexico and 1 – Chiapas

The data used to perform this regression are cross-sectional data from the Mexican Population Census. Note that a Tobit model is deployed given that income data are censored at the top (income at and above P\$ 999,999 recorded at P\$ 999,9999 in the data set).

Equation (2) is used to construct the return to schooling at each year of schooling after generating the average year of experience held by individuals at each year of schooling.

$$Log\_return_{year} = \alpha + \beta_1 * years\ of\ schooling + \beta_2 * AVERAGE_{years\ of\ experience}$$
$$+\beta_3 * (AVERAGE_{yearsofexperience})^2 + \beta_6 * Chiapas.$$
$$Equation(2)$$

The results of regression – equation (1) – is reported in Table 2.

Table 2 Mincer regression for Mexico and Chiapas

	Income (1)	Income (2)
Schooling	0.0978***	0.0970***
	(0.000336)	(0.000329)
Experience	0.0328***	0.0326***
	(0.000105)	(0.000105)
Experience squared	−0.000441***	−0.000439***
	(1.78e-06)	(1.77e-06)
Female	−0.334***	−0.336***
	(0.00134)	(0.00130)
Indigenous language	−0.277***	−0.259***
	(0.00877)	(0.00775)
Chiapas		−0.358***
		(0.0121)
Constant	7.113***	7.133***
	(0.00382)	(0.00367)
Observations	2,965,928	2,965,928

Note: Standard errors are shown in parentheses. ***$p < 0.01$, **$p < 0.05$, and *$p < 0.1$.

Source: 10 percent Microdata sample of 2010 Population Census (National Institute of Statistics and Geography [INEGI]).

Appendix 2
Incorporating Quality in Mincer Regression

Adjusting the estimated Mincerian return to schooling by schooling quality is a two-step endeavor. The first step is to establish an acceptable measure of schooling quality (step 1), and the next step is to estimate the relationship between income and schooling and schooling quality while controlling for a number of variables (step 2).

Step 1: Measuring Quality of Schooling

In the case of Mexico, the Ministry of Education runs the ENLACE to measure proficiency in Math and Spanish language of students in public and private schools, at all pre-college levels: primary, secondary, and media superior (last grade). The results of the test are reported at the locality level. This has two important implications: First, as the data are reported at the level of localities, it is then possible to estimate the relative quality of schooling for each municipality in each state. Second, as the test is taken by students at all pre-college levels, it is possible to compare the relative quality of schooling by the level of schooling.

As quality measures, the practitioner has the option of using raw test scores by municipality/state.

Another option is to estimate the relationship between test scores and observed characteristics at the state, municipality, and household levels to isolate the quality component from the test scores. The rationale being that test scores are unlikely to only reflect the quality of schooling students are receiving. Instead, test scores are affected by a number of variables, such as family income and parents' highest level of schooling; in the case of Mexico, ethnic background is also part of the variables that may affect students' schooling outcomes.

This second option requires merging the test score data with the Mexican Population Census and using an OLS regression model to estimate the relationship between the ENLACE test scores and these variables, using the following regression:

$$test\ score_{municipality;schooling\ level} = \alpha + \beta_1 * years\ of\ schooling$$
$$+ \beta_2 * family\ income$$
$$+ \beta_3 * maximum\ family\ schooling$$
$$+ \beta_4 * Indigenous language + \varepsilon,$$

$$Equation(3)$$

where ε captures the quality of schooling, being the difference between the observed test score and the predicted test score, based on observed characteristics, such as years of schooling and family profile. Hence, we use equation (4) to estimate quality (ε).

$$\varepsilon_{municipality;schoolinglevel} = testscore_{(m;s)} - predictedtestscore_{(m,s)}, \qquad \text{Equation}(4)$$

where *Predictedtestscore$_i$* is the test score estimated by substituting for the variable and regression coefficients in equation (3).

Step 2: Incorporating Quality of Schooling in the Mincer Regression

A Tobit model or censored regression model is used to estimate the relationship between income and years of schooling, adjusted quality of schooling, as modeled in equation (5). The purpose is to estimate the Mincerian returns on an additional year of schooling in Chiapas versus the rest of Mexico, adjusted for schooling quality in each state. This regression can be estimated at a state or municipal level, depending on available data.

$$
\begin{aligned}
Log_{income_{(person\ at\ m,s\ levels)}} == & \ \alpha + \beta_1 * years\ of\ schooling_{person} \\
& +\beta_2 * years\ of\ experience_{person} \\
& +\beta_3 * \left(years\ of\ experience_{person}\right)^2 \\
& +\beta_4 * quality_{spanish\ (at\ m,s\ levels)} \\
& +\beta_5 * quality_{math\ (at\ m,s\ levels)} \\
& +\beta_6 * Chiapas, \qquad \text{Equation}(5)
\end{aligned}
$$

where *Quality$_{spanish}$* and *Quality$_{math}$* are quality measure computed using the test scores of ENLACE Spanish and Math components, respectively. Both quality measures are calculated according to step 1.

The regression results of equation (5) are reported in *Table 3*.

Equation (6) is used to construct the expected wage schedule in each state (our variable of interest), adjusted for schooling quality, each level of schooling:

$$
\begin{aligned}
Log_{return_{state,year}} = & \ \alpha + \beta_1 * yearsofschooling + \beta_2 * \\
& AVERAGEyearsofexperience_{atstateandschoolinglevel} + \beta_3 * \\
& \left(AVERAGE_{years}ofexperience_{atstateandschoolinglevel}\right)^2 + \beta_4 * \\
& quality_{spanish;atstateandschoolinglevels} + \beta_5 * quality_{math;atstateandschoolinglevels} + \beta_6 * \\
& Chiapas.
\end{aligned}
$$

$$\text{Equation}(6)$$

Table 3 Mincer regression in Mexico and Chiapas – adjusted for quality of schooling

	Chiapas = 1 (1)	Chiapas = 0 (2)
Schooling	0.0989 (0.002302)***	0.0765 (0.000323)***
Experience	0.0306 (0.000665)***	0.0339 (0.000114)***
Experience squared	−0.0004015 (0.00001)***	−0.000493 $(1.98*10^\wedge-6)$***
Quality$_{Spanish}$	0.21861 (0.01421)***	0.13128 (0.00329)***
Quality$_{Math}$	−0.1202 (0.01706)***	−0.0507 (0.00346)***
Constant	6.589 (0.03512)***	7.1505 (0.00387)***
Observations	511,079	7,281,494

Note: Standard errors are shown in parentheses. ***$p < 0.01$, **$p < 0.05$, and *$p < 0.1$.

Note on schooling quality at the state level: Quality at state and schooling levels can be calculated as per step 1. Alternatively, the quality at municipality and schooling levels can be used to aggregate at the state level, by taking the average quality (in Spanish and Math) across municipalities, at each level of schooling.

Appendix 3

Wage Premiums by Industry and Occupation

A simple OLS regression model is used to estimate the wage premium on foreign labor in a given country, modeled according to equation (7). A representative micro-level labor force survey, reporting wages, demographics, educational attainments, occupations, is needed to estimate the following equation:

$$Log\_income_{state,year} = \alpha + \beta_1 * foreign + \beta_2 * female$$
$$+ \beta_3 * schooling + \beta_4 * occupation$$
$$+ \beta_5 * industry + \sum \beta_i X_i, \qquad \text{Equation}(7)$$

- *Foreign* – a dummy variable: 1 – foreign workers and 0 – national workers
- *Female* – a dummy variable for gender: 1 – female and 0 – male
- *Schooling* – a continuous variable for years of schooling; it might also be a categorical variable indicating a certain level of school (0 – illiterate, 1 – primary schooling, 2 – secondary schooling, 3 – tertiary, and 4 – PhD)
- *Occupation* – a categorical variable referring to individuals' occupation type, for example, 1 – managers, 2 – professionals, 3 – technicians, 4 – clerks, and so on (not included in the regression when estimating the wage premiums by occupation)
- *Industry* – a categorical variable referring to the industry in which individuals work (not included in the regression when estimating the wage premiums by industry)
- $\sum \beta_i X_i$ – a matrix of other observable characteristics that may influence income, such as age, experience, region of the country, and so on.

The Wage Premium

The wage premium of foreigners by industry is β_1, when equation (7) is estimated by industry. The wage premium of foreigners by occupation is β_1, when equation (7) is estimated by occupation.

By capturing β_1, as well as the standard error of term β_1, the practitioner is able to estimate the lower and upper bounds of foreigners' wage premiums, relative to national labor, according to equation (8):

Lower bound of foreigner wage premium$_{by\ industry\ or\ occupation}$ $= \beta_1 - 1.96$
$* standard error on foreigner coefficient(β_1), $\qquad \text{Equation}(8)$

Appendix 4

Industry Factor Intensity and Relationship to Country Exports

A simple OLS regression model is used to model the relationship between a country's exports and the country's industry factor intensity (i.e., industry specialization in skills or physical capital). The goal is to estimate the contribution of skill- versus capital-intensive industries to a country's exports. A comparison of the contribution of skill- and capital-intensive industries to exports is informative of whether agents in the economy (firms) are moving away from or toward industries intensive in a aaparticular factor. This can reveal a comparative advantage in leveraging a factor or can reveal constraints in the factor firms move away from.

We leverage the database made available by Nunn (2007) to demonstrate the example of South Africa in Section 2.4. The database includes disaggregated country export and import data, at the three-digit product level for the year 1997, an industry skill measure based on prevalent wages of the sector, capital stock per worker for each sector. We do not elaborate on the mechanics of constructing the skill and capital per worker measures of the sectors; these are estimated according to input-output tables reported by the US Bureau of Economic Analysis, by industry classification.

The OLS model is based on equation (9) presented below and is estimated separately for each factor (skills vs. capital):

$$\frac{Exports_{industry,country}}{Total exports_{country}} = \alpha + \beta_c * FACTOR_{INTENSITY_{industry}}$$
$$+ \beta_1 * D_{industry} * \ln\left(Total exports_{country}\right)$$
$$+ \beta_3 * D_{industry} + \beta_4 * D_{country}$$
$$+ \varepsilon_{i,c}. \qquad\qquad \text{Equation}(9)$$

- $\frac{Exports_{industry,country}}{Total exports_{country}}$ – the dependent variable is an industry's share of country exports. This can also be substituted for, by an industry's share in gross value added. This variable is unique for each industry i, in a country c.
- *FACTOR INSTENSITY* – a continuous variable of the industry's factor intensity. In regressions estimating skill intensity, this would be the variable indicating an industry's skill intensity. In regressions estimating capital

intensity, this variable would indicate the industry's capital stock per worker. This variable is unique to the industry.

- $D_{industry}$ – a categorical dummy variable for industries. For the purposes of this model, we use industry six-digit codes to encode the industries' ordinal (dummy) variable.
- $D_{country}$ – a categorical dummy variable for countries. We rely on country ISO codes to produce this variable for each country.
- *Total export $_{country}$* – a continuous variable of a country's total product exports, in log levels. We assume that richer countries are likely to have stronger patterns of factor specialization. To account for this association between a country's level of development and its factor intensity, we use a country's total exports as a control variable for the country's wealth level. This can also be substituted for by using GDP per capita.

Ideally, the above model aims to detect significant positive or negative β_c coefficients. A positive β_c coefficient implies that industries more intensive in the factor under consideration (skills or capital in this case) are associated with a greater share of the country's exports, controlling for the country's level of wealth. This suggests that industries intensive in the factor under study are thriving. On the other hand, a negative β_c coefficient indicates that industries more intensive in the factor under study are associated with a lower share of the country's exports. This suggests these industries contribute less to country exports and hence may be struggling to grow.

In the example of South Africa discussed in Section 2.4, the β_c coefficient, for both regressions modeling the relationship between exports and industries' skill intensity as well as capital intensity, is not statistically significant for comparator countries: Brazil, Chile, Colombia, Mexico, and Indonesia. Therefore, for these countries, we cannot infer a relationship significantly different than zero between industries' skill intensity and these industries' share of exports and similarly between industries' capital intensity and their share in exports. Meanwhile, the β_c coefficients, in both skill- and capital-intensity regressions, are significant for South Africa. The higher an industry's skill intensity is, the lower its share of South Africa's exports is, whereas the higher an industry's capital intensity is, the greater its share of South Africa's exports is. These respective negative and positive relationships are statistically significant, providing evidence that there is reason to believe South Africa's industries could be specializing away from industries dependent on skills and preferring activities that rely predominantly on machines.

References

Angrist, N. *et al.* (2019) *Measuring Human Capital*. Washington, DC: World Bank. Available at SSRN 3339416.

Antweiler, W. and Trefler, D. (2002) "Increasing returns and all that: a view from trade," *American Economic Review*, 92(1), pp. 93–119.

Banerjee, A. *et al.* (2008) "Why has unemployment risen in the new South Africa? 1," *Economics of Transition*, 16(4), pp. 715–740.

Bartelsman, E. J. and Gray, W. (1996) *The NBER Manufacturing Productivity Database*. Technical working paper 205. Cambridge, MA: National Bureau of Economic Research.

Becker, G. S. (1962) "Investment in human capital: A theoretical analysis," *Journal of Political Economy*, 70(5, Part 2), pp. 9–49.

Becker, G. S. (2007) "Health as human capital: synthesis and extensions," *Oxford Economic Papers*, 59(3), pp. 379–410.

Becker, G. S. and Chiswick, B. R. (1966) "Education and the distribution of earnings," *The American Economic Review*, 56(1/2), pp. 358–369.

Bernard, M. and Ravenhill, J. (1995) "Beyond product cycles and flying geese: regionalization, hierarchy, and the industrialization of East Asia," *World Politics*, 47(2), pp. 171–209.

Bils, M. and Klenow, P. J. (2000) "Does schooling cause growth?," *American Economic Review*, 90(5), pp. 1160–1183.

Blundell, R., Bozio, A. and Laroque, G. (2011) "Labor supply and the extensive margin," *American Economic Review*, 101(3), pp. 482–486.

Bosworth, B. and Collins, S. M. (2003) "The empirics of growth: An update," *Brookings Papers on Economic Activity*, 2003(2), pp. 113–206.

Card, D. (1999) 'Chapter 30 – The Causal Effect of Education on Earnings', in Ashenfelter, O. C. and Card, D. (eds) *Handbook of Labor Economics*. Amsterdam: Elsevier, pp. 1801–1863. doi:10.1016/S1573-4463(99)03011-4.

Caselli, F. (2005) "Accounting for cross-country income differences," *Handbook of Economic Growth*, 1, pp. 679–741.

Comisión Nacional de Productividad | Informe Anual (2016) *La productividad en Chile: Una mirada de largo plazo*. Available at: www.comisiondeproductivi dad.cl/2017/12/26/informe-anual-2016-la-productividad-en-chile-una-mir ada-de-largo-plazo/ (Accessed: July 23, 2021).

Enterprise Surveys, –World Bank. Available at: www.enterprisesurveys.org/en/ enterprisesurveys (Accessed: June 29, 2020).

Hall, R. E. and Jones, C. I. (1999) "Why do some countries produce so much more output per worker than others?," *The Quarterly Journal of Economics*, 114(1), pp. 83–116.

Hausmann, R. *et al.* (2019) *Jordan: The Elements of a Growth Strategy*. CID Working Paper Series. Cambridge, MA: Harvard University

Hausmann, R., Espinoza, L. and Santos, M. A. (2015) "The Low Productivity Trap: Chiapas Growth Diagnostics," *Harvard University: Center for International Development Working Paper*, (304).

Hausmann, R., Klinger, B. and Wagner, R. (2008) Doing Growth Diagnostics in Practice: a "Mindbook." *CID Working Paper Series*. Cambridge, MA: Harvard University.

Hausmann, R., Obach, J. and Santos, M. (2016) "Special Economic Zones in Panama: A critical assessment," *CID Working Papers 326*, Center for International Development at Harvard University.

Hausmann, R., Pan, C. and Santos, M. A. (2020) *The Chiapas Puzzle*. HKS Case Number: 2174.0, p. 23. Available at: https://case.hks.harvard.edu/the-chiapas-puzzle/ (Accessed: July 22, 2021).

Hausmann, R., Pietrobelli, C. and Santos, M. A. (2018) "Place-specific Determinants of Income Gaps: New Sub-National Evidence from Chiapas, Mexico," *CID Working Paper Series No. 343*.

Hausmann, R., Pietrobelli, C. and Santos, M. A. (2021) "Place-specific determinants of income gaps: New sub-national evidence from Mexico," *Journal of Business Research*. https://doi.org/10.1016/j.jbusres.2021.01.003.

Hausmann, R., Rodrik, D. and Velasco, A. (2008) "Growth Diagnostics," in Stiglitz, J.E. and Serra, N. (eds) *The Washington Consensus Reconsidered: Towards a New Global Governance*. United Kingdom: Oxford University Press. pp. 324–355.

Heckman, J. J., Lochner, L. J. and Todd, P. E. (2003) *Fifty Years of Mincer Earnings Regressions*. Cambridge, MA: National Bureau of Economic Research.

Javorcik, B. S. and Spatareanu, M. (2008) "To share or not to share: Does local participation matter for spillovers from foreign direct investment?," *Journal of Development Economics*, 85(1), pp. 194–217. http://doi.org/10.1016/j.jdeveco.2006.08.005.

Kaffenberger, M. and Pritchett, L. (2017) "More school or more learning? Evidence from learning profiles from the financial inclusion insights data," *World Development Report Background Paper*. Washington, DC: World Bank.

Kaffenberger, M. and Pritchett, L. (2020) "Women's Education May Be Even Better Than We Thought: Estimating the Gains from Education When

Schooling Ain't Learning," *RISE Working Paper Series. 2020/049.* Available at: https://doi.org/10.35489/BSG-RISE-WP_2020/049.

Kasahara, S. (2004) "The Flying Geese Paradigm: A critical study of its application to East Asian regional development." Geneva: UNCTAD, United Nations Conference of Trade and Development. Discussion Paper: 169.

Kasoolu, S. *et al.* (2019) "Female Labor in Jordan: A Systematic Approach to the Exclusion Puzzle." *CID Working Paper Series.* Cambridge, MA: Harvard University.

Kojima, K. (2000) "The 'flying geese' model of Asian economic development: origin, theoretical extensions, and regional policy implications," *Journal of Asian Economics*, 11(4), pp. 375–401.

Levinsohn, J. A. (2008) *Two policies to alleviate unemployment in South Africa.* Center for International Development at Harvard University.

"Look Beyond Basics: Annual Status Education Report" (2017) ASER centre. Pratham. Safdarjung, New Delhi. Available at: http://img.asercentre.org /docs/Publications/ASER%20Reports/ASER%202017/aser2017fullreportf inal.pdf

Lucas, R. (1988) "On the mechanics of development planning," *Journal of Monetary Economics*, 22(1), pp. 3–42.

Mankiw, N. G., Romer, D. and Weil, D. N. (1992) "A contribution to the empirics of economic growth," *The Quarterly Journal of Economics*, 107 (2), pp. 407–437.

McKenzie, D. (2017) "How effective are active labor market policies in developing countries? A critical review of recent evidence," *The World Bank Research Observer*, 32(2), pp. 127–154.

Michau, J.-B. (2011) "Optimal Redistribution with Intensive and Extensive Labor Supply Margins: A Life-Cycle Perspective." Available at: https://hal .archives-ouvertes.fr/hal-00639121 (Accessed: September 27, 2020).

Mincer, J. (1958) "Investment in human capital and personal income distribution," *Journal of Political Economy*, 66(4), pp. 281–302.

Mincer, J. (1974) *Schooling, Earnings and Experience.* New York: Columbia University Press.

Mincer, J. (1984) "Human capital and economic growth," *Economics of Education Review*, 3(3), pp. 195–205.

Myrdal, G. and Sitohang, P. (1957) "Economic Theory and Underdeveloped Regions. London: Duckworth.

Nunn, N. (2007) "Relationship-specificity, incomplete contracts, and the pattern of trade," *The Quarterly Journal of Economics*, 122(2), pp. 569–600.

OAMDI (2017) "Harmonized Labor Force Surveys (HLFS), http://erf/org/eg/ data-portal/. Version 1.0 of Licensed Data Files; EUS 2016 – Department of

Statistics (DOS), The Hashemite Kingdom of Jordan." Egypt: Economic Research Forum (ERF).

Patrinos, H. A. (2016) "Estimating the return to schooling using the Mincer equation," *IZA World of Labor* 2016: 278 doi: 10.15185/izawol.278.

PISA – PISA (no date). Available at: www.oecd.org/pisa/ (Accessed: July 10, 2020).

Pizarro, A. *et al.* (2016) "Third Regional Comparative and Explanatory Study (TERCE): Learning Achievements," *Latin American Laboratory for Assessment of the Quality of Education, UNESCO.* Volume 3.

Pritchett, L. (2006) "Does learning to add up add up? The returns to schooling in aggregate data," *Handbook of the Economics of Education*, 1, pp. 635–695.

Pritchett, L. (2013) *The Rebirth of Education: Schooling Ain't Learning.* Washington, DC: Center for Global Development.

Pritchett, L., Samji, S. and Hammer, J. S. (2013) "It's All About MeE: Using Structured Experiential Learning ('e') to Crawl the Design Space," *SSRN Electronic Journal.* http://doi.org/10.2139/ssrn.2248785.

Psacharopoulos, G. and Patrinos, H. A. (2018) "Returns to investment in education".

Rajan, R. and Zingales, L. (1998) "Financial development and growth," *American Economic Review*, 88(3), pp. 559–586.

Rhee, Y. W. (1990) "The catalyst model of development: Lessons from Bangladesh's success with garment exports," *World Development*, 18(2), pp. 333–346.

Romer, P. M. (1986) "Increasing Returns and Long-Run Growth," *Journal of Political Economy*, 94(5), pp. 1002–1037.

Rosen, S. (1988) "The value of changes in life expectancy," *Journal of Risk and Uncertainty*, 1(3), pp. 285–304.

Schultz, T. W. (1960) "Capital formation by education," *Journal of Political Economy*, 68(6), pp. 571–583.

Schultz, T. W. (1961) "Investment in human capital," *The American Economic Review*, 51(1), pp. 1–17.

Schultz, T. W. (1963) *The Economic Value of Education.* New York, NY: Columbia University Press.

Smith, A. (1776) *An Inquiry into the Nature and Causes of the Wealth of Nations.* Volume One," London: printed for W. Strahan; and T. Cadell, 1776.

Solow, R. M. (1956) "A contribution to the theory of economic growth," *The Quarterly Journal of Economics*, 70(1), pp. 65–94.

Subramanian, M. A. and Alleyne, M. T. S. C. (2001) *What Does South Africa's Pattern of Trade Say About its Labor Markets?* Washington, DC: International Monetary Fund (1–148).

Temple, J. (1999) "A positive effect of human capital on growth," *Economics Letters*, 65(1), pp. 131–134.

Uh, S. (2018) *Job Training in the Republic of Korea: Background Note for the South Africa Systematic Country Diagnostic*. Washington, DC: World Bank.

United Nations Economic Commission for Europe (UNECE). (2016) *Guide on Measuring Human Capital*. Geneva: United Nations. Available at: https://www.unece.org/fileadmin/DAM/stats/publications/2016/HumanCapitalGuide.web.pdf

United Nation Valdés, H. *et al.* (2008) "Student Achievement in Latin America and the Caribbean. Results of the Second Regional Comparative and Explanatory Study (SERCE)," *Santiago de Chile: UNESCO/Laboratorio Latinoamericano de Evaluación de la Calidad de la Educación*. Volume: 2

World bank. *Education Statistics| Learning Outcomes* (no date). Available at: http://datatopics.worldbank.org/education/wDashboard/dqlearning.

World Bank (2015) *Indonesia – Enterprise Survey (ES) 2015, Ref. IDN_2015_ES_v01_M*. Available at: https://datacatalog.worldbank.org/dataset/indonesia-enterprise-survey-2015 (Accessed: January 18, 2021).

World Bank Group (2018) *An Incomplete Transition: Overcoming the Legacy of Exclusion in South Africa*. Washington, DC: World Bank. doi:10.1596/29793. Available at: https://openknowledge.worldbank.org/handle/10986/29793

World Bank (2020) *The Human Capital Index 2020 Update: Human Capital in the Time of COVID-19*. Washington, DC: World Bank. doi:10.1596/34432. Available at: https://openknowledge.worldbank.org/handle/10986/34432

Acknowledgments

This work is made possible by the support of the US government through the Millennium Challenge Corporation (MCC). The contents are the responsibility of the Growth Lab and the authors and do not necessarily reflect the views of MCC or the US government or Harvard University.

The authors are grateful to Ricardo Hausmann, Lant Pritchett, Rodrigo Wagner, Patricio Goldstein Semiray Kasoolu, and Bailey Klinger for their helpful comments and suggestions. Thanks to the cohorts of Growth Lab Fellows, working on applied research projects across the globe, their work and creativity have been leveraged to illustrate the deployment of the principles of differential diagnosis in this paper. The usual disclaimers apply.

Cambridge Elements ≡

Economics of Emerging Markets

Bruno S. Sergi
Harvard University

Editor Bruno S. Sergi is an instructor at Harvard University and an associate of the Harvard University Davis Center for Russian and Eurasian Studies and Harvard Ukrainian Research Institute. He is the academic series editor of the Cambridge *Elements in the Economics of Emerging Markets* (Cambridge University Press), a co-editor of the *Lab for Entrepreneurship and Development* book series, and associate editor of *The American Economist*. Concurrently, he teaches international economics at the University of Messina, scientific director of the Lab for Entrepreneurship and Development, and a co-founder and scientific director of the International Center for Emerging Markets Research at RUDN University in Moscow. He has published over 150 articles in professional journals and 21 books as author, co-author, editor, and co-editor.

About the Series

The aim of this Elements series is to deliver state-of-the-art, comprehensive coverage of the knowledge developed to date, including the dynamics and prospects of these economies, focusing on emerging markets' economics, finance, banking, technology advances, trade, demographic challenges, and their economic relations with the rest of the world, as well as the causal factors and limits of economic policy in these markets.

Cambridge Elements ☰

Economics of Emerging Markets

Elements in the Series

A full series listing is available at: www.cambridge.org/EEM

Printed in the United States
by Baker & Taylor Publisher Services